NEW DIRECTIONS FOR INSTITUTIONAL RESEARCH

J. Fredericks Volkwein, *Pennsylvania State University*
EDITOR-IN-CHIEF

Larry H. Litten, *Consortium on Financing Higher Education,
Cambridge, Massachusetts*
ASSOCIATE EDITOR

A New Era of Alumni Research: Improving Institutional Performance and Better Serving Alumni

Joseph Pettit
Georgetown University

Larry H. Litten
Consortium on Financing Higher Education

EDITORS

Number 101, Spring 1999

JOSSEY-BASS PUBLISHERS
San Francisco

A NEW ERA OF ALUMNI RESEARCH: IMPROVING INSTITUTIONAL
PERFORMANCE AND BETTER SERVING ALUMNI
Joseph Pettit, Larry H. Litten (eds.)
New Directions for Institutional Research, no. 101
Volume XXVI, Number 1
J. Fredericks Volkwein, Editor-in-Chief

New Directions for Institutional Research is indexed in *College Student
Personnel Abstracts, Contents Pages in Education,* and *Current Index to Jour-
nals in Education* (ERIC).

Microfilm copies of issues and chapters are available in 16mm and 35mm,
as well as microfiche in 105mm, through University Microfilms Inc., 300
North Zeeb Road, Ann Arbor, Michigan 48106-1346.

ISSN 0271-0579   ISBN 0-7879-1407-X

NEW DIRECTIONS FOR INSTITUTIONAL RESEARCH is part of The Jossey-Bass
Higher and Adult Education Series and is published quarterly by Jossey-
Bass Inc., Publishers, 350 Sansome Street, San Francisco, California
94104-1342 (publication number USPS 098-830). Periodicals postage
paid at San Francisco, California, and at additional mailing offices. POST-
MASTER: Send address changes to New Directions for Institutional
Research, Jossey-Bass Inc., Publishers, 350 Sansome Street, San Francisco,
California 94104-1342.

SUBSCRIPTIONS cost $56.00 for individuals and $95.00 for institutions,
agencies, and libraries.

EDITORIAL CORRESPONDENCE should be sent to J. Fredericks Volkwein,
Center for the Study of Higher Education, Pennsylvania State University,
403 South Allen Street, Suite 104, University Park, PA 16801-5252.

Photograph of the library by Michael Graves at San Juan Capistrano by
Chad Slattery © 1984. All rights reserved.

www.josseybass.com

Printed in the United States of America on acid-free recycled paper con-
taining 100 percent recovered waste paper, of which at least 20 percent is
postconsumer waste.

*This volume of New Directions for Institutional Research
was a cooperative effort of the Association for Institutional Research
and the Council for the Advancement and Support of Education.*

CONTENTS

EDITORS' NOTES

Alumni play many roles in relation to the institutions of higher education from which they graduated. Colleges and universities actively engage their alumni in some roles. In other roles, alumni have an effect on their alma maters irrespective of immediate institutional involvement. Most four-year colleges and universities actively seek financial support from their alumni. Many institutions ask their alumni to participate in the process of student recruiting and in helping students find internships and employment. Alumni networks are one of the principal benefits that a college or university offers its graduates. Alumni constitute a core spectator group for many collegiate athletic programs. They are increasingly seen as a market for educational and other services.

Alumni serve as de facto representatives of a college or university whenever people associate them with their alma maters. Impressions of an institution are often first formed based on a person knowing one of the institution's graduates. (Conversely, people are often judged by what others know, or think they know, about the schools from which these individuals have graduated.) When alumni speak of their alma maters, their impact as representatives—as promoters or as critics—is even more direct. And when they vote or otherwise influence public policy, alumni have an effect on the well-being of an institution.

Traditional research on alumni has focused primarily on fundraising from alumni, with a secondary focus on how alumni associations can serve their members; however, these foci are too narrow. Any research on how alumni behave in the roles listed above and how institutional policies and practices contribute to, or impede, desirable behavior in these roles constitutes essential institutional research. Furthermore, colleges and universities are increasingly tapping alumni to provide critical assessments of the institution's performance in preparing students to lead productive and rewarding lives. In addition to seeking evaluations from other professional educators through accreditation and from current students through course evaluations and surveys, colleges and universities are asking alumni to evaluate their educational experiences. Unlike faculty and current students, alumni bring the advantage of having tested the outcomes of an educational program in the marketplace. Alumni also have a critical interest in having their alma maters be as strong as possible and having them viewed positively and are therefore willing contributors to these evaluation processes.

Alumni research can focus on what an institution has done for alumni (the outcomes it has produced or facilitated), what it can do for alumni (the services they want), how the alumni view the institution and what it did for them, or how alumni can serve the institution more effectively. In addition to providing information of intrinsic value, alumni research also demonstrates an institutional commitment to self-understanding (a component of accountability). Furthermore, alumni research is itself a mechanism through which positive alumni relations are cultivated—people like to be taken seriously and listened to.

The various roles that alumni play in the life of an institution and the several foci for alumni research produce a wide internal audience for such research. Academic and student services administrators, public relations and development officers, as well as alumni affairs directors can all benefit from some kind of alumni research. The challenge is not finding sufficient things to study or audiences for research but rather setting priorities among many competing possibilities.

Knowing that there is a vast alumni research domain to be explored and that the most recent *New Directions for Institutional Research* volume on alumni research had appeared a decade ago, the editors of this volume decided it was time to revisit the territory. We elected to pursue our quest through two innovative means of compiling a collection of exemplary work. First, we asked the professional association for alumni affairs directors—the Council for the Advancement and Support of Education (CASE)—to assist us, as members of the Association for Institutional Research (AIR), in the search for appropriate research and in the selection of papers to become chapters in a *New Directions for Institutional Research* volume. An AIR-CASE collaboration assured that we would cast the widest possible net in identifying existing research, and it allowed us to increase the prospect that the researchers would learn about the concerns of the practitioners and that the practitioners would be able to learn what the researchers might offer them. Second, we decided to have potential contributors present their work at a conference where both institutional researchers and alumni affairs practitioners could critically review the work prior to publication. This increased the likelihood that the two groups would talk to, and not past, each other and that they would work together on forging new directions for the future of alumni research.

CASE and AIR both disseminated a call for papers for the conference through a variety of media. We asked for papers that addressed one or more of the following topics in Table 1.

We received twenty papers; a team of alumni affairs directors and institutional researchers selected seventeen for presentation at the conference (one author later withdrew). The foci of the papers that were submitted are shown on page 3.

The first AIR-CASE Conference on Alumni Research was held at Georgetown University on April 3 and April 4, 1998, and was attended by 106 people. Sixteen papers were presented in pairs; an institutional researcher and an alumni affairs director discussed each paper before the audience joined in the discussion. The give-and-take across the professions was exhilarating. It became clear, however, that the two groups brought distinctive sets of concerns to the table and that continued conversations would be essential if the most fruitful relationships were to develop and alumni research were to advance sufficiently

Table 1. Proposals for Papers

Topics	Number of Proposals Submitted
Services for alumni	1
Alumni volunteer service to institutions	2
Using alumni to assess institutions, programs, policies	12
Fundraising from alumni	10
Using alumni in the political process	0
Models of alumni-institutional relations	1
Sociocultural analysis of alumni groups	4
Organizing, supporting, conducting research on alumni	5
Evaluating alumni offices and programs	1
Other research related to alumni	1

Note: Sums to more than 20 because of multiple foci.

to realize its considerable potential. We hope that this volume will help advance these discussions more widely within and between the two professions.

Apart from producing the material for this *New Directions for Institutional Research* volume, which was its original objective, the conference has had a much broader impact. The president of CASE, Eustace Theodore, announced at the concluding session that the Georgetown conference would be the first in a series of annual collaborative conferences sponsored by CASE and AIR on research related to the professional concerns of CASE—alumni affairs, communications, and fundraising. The two organizations also pledged to work on other means of advancing the execution and application of research related to these three areas.

Selecting a few papers for publication in this volume from the many fine papers that were presented at the conference was a major challenge. (A synopsis of all the papers and the discussion can be found in the CASE publication *Research in Alumni Relations: Report on the 1998 AIR-CASE Alumni Research Conference, item 28124.*) The task of selecting papers for this volume was performed by a team of institutional researchers and alumni affairs personnel. We endeavored to select papers that present a variety of foci, research methods, and sponsorship. Thus, we have research that looks at services for alumni (Chapter Two), fundraising from alumni (Chapters One, Two, and Four), alumni and employer evaluations of a college's curricula (Chapter Three), an assessment of the impact of an undergraduate program designed to strengthen alumni ties to an institution (Chapter Four), and the occupational and other outcomes of college (Chapter Five). The research was conducted via focus group (Chapter One), phone surveys (Chapters One and Two), mail surveys (Chapters Three, Four, and Five), and institutional data analysis (Chapter Two). The research was conducted by researchers from development and alumni offices (Chapters One and Two), institutional research offices (Chapters Three and Four), a market research firm (Chapter Two), and a state association research center (Chapter Five).

We would like to thank the many people who contributed to the process that produced this volume, especially the presidents of the two organizations that sponsored the conference, Eustace Theodore (CASE) and Mary Sapp (AIR); the executive director of AIR, Terry Russell; the vice president for alumni affairs at CASE, Paul Chewning; and the director of the information center at CASE, Barbara Perkins. We also greatly appreciate the contributions made by the twenty-four people who produced the sixteen papers that were presented at the conference and the twenty-four individuals who discussed these papers; their names can be found in the CASE volume cited above.

Joseph Pettit
Larry H. Litten
Editors

JOSEPH PETTIT is vice president for planning and institutional research and the class of '64 communications chair at Georgetown University.

LARRY H. LITTEN is associate director and director of research at the Consortium on Financing Higher Education.

By reviewing some of the alumni research conducted at Stanford University—and how the findings have been used—this chapter indicates the range of development and alumni relations issues for which market research can be valuable. The chapter also demonstrates the benefits of conducting ongoing, as opposed to occasional, research.

Comprehensive Research on Alumni Relationships: Four Years of Market Research at Stanford University

Jerold Pearson

In 1992, Stanford University concluded its five-year centennial campaign by exceeding its fundraising goal of $1.1 billion. Nevertheless, the Office of Development (and the university's new president) were disappointed at the minimal amount of unrestricted funds at the president's disposal and were dissatisfied that Stanford lacked a strong tradition of annual giving. The Office of Development therefore made unrestricted annual giving a higher priority than it had previously been and began to invest more attention and resources in its annual giving programs. It redefined its various undergraduate and graduate annual funds, more clearly delineated the populations that each fund could solicit (to eliminate inappropriate multiple solicitations), and provided each fund with staff that was responsible and accountable for results. It employed more effective methods of soliciting annual gifts—by modernizing its telephone-calling facilities, switching from volunteer callers to well-trained paid student callers, and better coordinating phone appeals with the direct mail programs. Most important for this discussion, it made a serious commitment to enhance its understanding of the populations it was soliciting.

Like most experienced fundraisers, Stanford's vice president for development understood that philanthropic support for an institution depends, to a large extent, on the relationships it has with its prospects. Unlike many others, he decided to examine those relationships with the rigor and objectivity afforded by professionally conducted market research. Unlike *almost all* others, he created a full-time position to conduct this research on an ongoing basis.

NEW DIRECTIONS FOR INSTITUTIONAL RESEARCH, no. 101, Spring 1999 © Jossey-Bass Publishers

Research itself is certainly not alien to fundraisers. Most colleges and universities do some sort of "prospect research" to understand, enhance, and respond to the relationships they have with *individuals* targeted for major and principal gifts. It is surprising then that so few conduct market research to understand, enhance, and respond to the relationships they have with *populations* targeted for annual gifts. It is even more surprising considering that market research has proven for almost a century to be a valuable tool, with high return on investment, in most other sectors of society.

Simply put, market research—especially when designed to produce actionable, rather than merely descriptive, data—enables strategy and tactics to be informed by valid and reliable measurements rather than by anecdote, speculation, and personal bias.

By reviewing some of the studies I have conducted for Stanford since my position was created in 1994, this chapter will indicate the range of development issues for which market research can be valuable. Furthermore, by noting how the findings have been used and how the insights gained from one study have suggested other issues to explore, it will demonstrate the benefits of ongoing, as opposed to occasional, research. Indeed, the findings from the initial study of undergraduate alumni giving have led to more focused research on graduate alumni giving, alumni relations, university communications, and even student affairs and community relations.

For instance, in addition to those discussed in this chapter, studies conducted by this office include a survey of alumni of color; a multi-institutional comparative survey; fundraising research for the athletics department; studies to suggest new marketing strategies for Stanford football, the Continuing Studies Program, and the Committee for Art; surveys for the Stanford Channel to measure viewership and its influence on perceptions of Stanford; a study on the college selection process from the parents' perspective; readership research for *Stanford* magazine; and a study to better understand alumni relations and development issues unique to alumni living in Asia.

Studies that were in progress or in the planning stage at the time this chapter was written include research with students designed to identify the factors that drive satisfaction with the undergraduate experience; surveys on community perceptions of Stanford's hospitals and medical center; a study of communications with parents; research with lapsed donors to understand why they do not renew their support to The Stanford Fund; and studies on membership issues, events programming, and program evaluations for the Stanford Alumni Association.

Initial Research on Undergraduate Alumni Giving

Considerable thought has been given to understanding the reasons why alumni make gifts to their alma mater, but because only 25 percent of undergraduate degree holders made a gift to Stanford's annual fund in 1993, my first study, conducted in the spring of 1994, explored the other side of the equation to learn why most alumni do *not* make gifts. The research was designed around the hypothesis that the decision to give is like a purchase decision: just as a consumer makes an active decision to buy a product for specific reasons, so too does the consumer make an active decision *not* to buy a different product for specific reasons (even if those reasons are emotional or based on misperceptions). One objective of this study was to discover those reasons so they could be addressed. Although the gains in alumni giving are due to various factors in addition to the research, it is worth noting that the undergraduate participation rate at Stanford has since risen each year, from 25 percent in 1993 to 34 percent in 1997.

Based on six focus groups followed by a telephone survey of 642 randomly selected undergraduate degree holders, this initial study measured aspects of alumni awareness, perceptions, and attitudes. It also tested a wide range of fundraising messages. Not surprisingly, the study confirmed that the relationship alumni have with Stanford plays a paramount role in their gift-making decision: alumni are more likely to be donors if they are very satisfied with their student experiences, if they are involved and engaged as alumni with the university, and if they are kept informed about what is happening at Stanford. Simply put, the stronger the relationship, the more likely they are to be donors. But for the first time, the components of the relationship were quantified, and those most in need of attention were identified. Just as important, the study also demonstrated the *interdependence* of the components: alumni who are most satisfied with their student experience are the most likely to remain engaged with the university; alumni who are most engaged are the most likely to read communications from the university; and those alumni who are most informed about the university are the most likely to remain engaged.

In short, the solicitation is the last event in a chain of events, and the decision to give (or not to give) is influenced by many things that occur long before the solicitation arrives. The correlations in the data strongly indicated that fundraising efforts can be more successful when student affairs, alumni relations, university communications, and development are interrelated and work closely with one another. Although this may seem obvious, it sent a very strong message to Stanford, where the university had little role in alumni relations (because of an independent alumni association) and where development had little say in university communications. Supported by the strong evidence provided by the research, the university and the alumni association have since agreed to merge, and development has obtained a stronger voice in communications and alumni relations.

The relationship that alumni have with the university begins with their experience as students and, not surprisingly, satisfaction with the student experience is the single most essential precondition for giving. Stanford alumni who are not satisfied with their student experience are, almost without exception, nondonors. Fortunately for Stanford, however, almost all alumni (97 percent) are satisfied with their student experience, and more than three-quarters are very satisfied. This finding, which has been replicated in every subsequent survey of Stanford alumni, is very reassuring in light of the low *alumni satisfaction* rating assigned to Stanford by *U.S. News & World Report*—a rating that is egregiously flawed, if not entirely mistaken, because it makes the error of partially equating satisfaction with gift giving. Satisfaction is a necessary *but not sufficient* condition for giving. One can be satisfied (and even *very* satisfied) with one's alma mater and still not make a gift to it. Giving is influenced also by the quality of alumni relations and communications, the perceived need of the institution, and the messages conveyed in solicitations—not to mention the methods used and the resources invested in fundraising.

There are, however, significant differences between alumni who are *very* satisfied with their student experience and those who are anything less than very satisfied. The survey showed that those who are very satisfied perceive the value of their Stanford education to be greater, take greater pride in their Stanford degree, have a stronger personal commitment to Stanford, and are more likely to be donors.

One of the most revealing findings of the research indicates that satisfaction is greater among alumni who feel that the best features of their education were *deliberately* provided by Stanford and that the quality of their education was achieved by the university's design rather than by chance. For instance, satisfaction was greatest among alumni who are most satisfied with the advising they received, who feel the university made them aware of the best classes and academic opportunities, and who were most challenged (academically and intellectually) by their undergraduate program.

The second component of the alumni relationship is the degree to which they are engaged with and involved in the life of the university. And just about every such measure in the survey indicated that the relationship alumni have with Stanford falters badly in this regard. Although this identified a major challenge that Stanford must address, it came with a silver lining. Anecdotal information had caused serious concern that many alumni withhold gifts to Stanford because they are angry at it for social and political reasons. However, the quantitative data from this—and every subsequent—survey strongly indicated that, with the exception of a small (older) minority, political issues play a minimal role in deterring alumni from making gifts. Most alumni are simply disengaged from—*not* disaffected with—Stanford.

Indeed, most alumni have positive feelings about Stanford; and, as the focus groups revealed, most of those with doubts are eager to be reassured that things are on the right track. Even the crankiest and most skeptical alumni appreciate that the world is changing and recognize that the university must change with it. What they want, however, is reason to believe that change is being managed in a thoughtful and judicious fashion, that the university has a clear direction and is not just blown by social and political winds. This insight helps explain why the quantitative data demonstrated that—regardless of age or other demographics—the more alumni know about the president's goals and priorities, the more favorable their perceptions of the university are, and the more likely they are to be donors. The importance of communicating effectively with alumni cannot be overstated.

Here again, the research strongly indicated that Stanford faces a challenge it must address. Alumni in the focus groups expressed frustration with communications that they felt were random, insufficiently salient to their interests, and not written from an alumni perspective. The survey data indicated that readership of the main alumni newspaper was moderate at best and that most alumni had little awareness of Stanford as it is now or of the issues the university considers most important to its future. Nevertheless, alumni do form perceptions of Stanford. To a great extent, however, those perceptions are formed more from vague impressions gleaned from outside sources than from information provided by the university. Like any successfully marketed product or program, a university must define itself to its audience rather than allow itself to be defined by others. Indeed, alumni who were most informed about Stanford *from Stanford sources* had more positive perceptions of it and were more likely to be donors.

The research suggested that Stanford would benefit from a comprehensive and coordinated communications strategy, which would ensure that communications with alumni are strategically timed rather than occasional and fortuitous, designed to articulate consistent messages, developed with alumni interests in mind, and informed by clear objectives.

If the findings concerning the alumni relationship can be considered strategic (or long-term) in nature, the study also provided tactical (or more immediately actionable) information—by identifying fundraising messages that do and do not resonate with Stanford alumni, and by revealing issues that need to be addressed because they deter alumni from making gifts. This information has since been used to craft more effective appeals and enhance fundraising efforts.

The study found that three of the messages being used at the time simply fall flat with most Stanford alumni, who do not respond to these suggestions of why they should support the university:

1. Tuition does not cover the cost of a Stanford education, and even those alumni who paid full tuition were subsidized. (The survey data indicated that this message is not compelling, and the focus groups explained why: it does more to raise negative questions about the ever rising cost of a Stanford education than it does to engender feelings of gratitude or indebtedness.)

2. Their gifts help Stanford provide the great teaching and stimulating classes from which they benefited. (To the contrary, many younger alumni recall—accurately or not—a much different experience, one that included large classes, little access to faculty, and too many teaching assistants.)

3. They have an obligation to Stanford. (Most Stanford alumni do not believe they have such an obligation, and many resent suggestions that they do.)

Nevertheless, alumni do feel that Stanford had a positive impact on their lives, and the main reason they consider making gifts is simply to give something back. But this alone is not enough to impel them to do so. Stanford must also demonstrate that what they give back will be used in meaningful ways. The research suggested that the most persuasive messages demonstrate the *impact* of alumni gifts—on individuals (through financial aid), on the university (by helping fund teaching initiatives and new programs), and on the world we live in (because Stanford is a leader in science, humanities, medicine, and technology).

In 1994, polls and social research consistently indicated that Americans thought most of their institutions were rife with bureaucratic waste and nonessential programs, and they distrusted administrators to spend funds wisely. Fortunately, alumni did not feel that way about Stanford, and these concerns play a minimal role in deterring them from making gifts to the university. Rather, the single greatest deterrent to making a gift to Stanford is the perception that it simply does not need their gifts as much as other organizations do. Most alumni believe that Stanford is not only a wealthy institution but also one that can always count on other sources for *major* funding. Furthermore, alumni feel their money has greater impact on smaller organizations and causes.

The perceptions of low need and lack of impact are the primary deterrents for all Stanford alumni and are even taken into consideration by donors. No other issue plays much of a deterrent role among younger alumni, but a secondary deterrent for older alumni is concern that Stanford has strayed from its core mission and values. Although, as previously noted, there is little anger at Stanford over social and political issues, some older alumni do question whether they can support what they perceive to be the university's misdirection.

Research with Graduate Alumni

After the initial study of undergraduate alumni, studies for most of Stanford's graduate schools were conducted. These studies explored issues unique to each school, but the consistency of the fundamental findings was remarkable: they indicated that Stanford's main challenges with graduate alumni are the same as those with undergraduate alumni. At each of the graduate schools, satisfaction with and perceived value of the student experience were quite high, whereas engagement and awareness were very low. Furthermore, the messages that most persuade alumni to give to the schools were all the same, as were the concerns that deter them.

The study for the School of Education (three focus groups followed by a telephone survey of 407 conducted in November 1994) was especially revealing because it strongly refuted the notion that alumni do not give to the school because they cannot afford to. In the first focus group, participants (most of whom were nondonors) were asked why they thought the vast majority of the school's alumni do not make gifts to it. Many immediately said that they were teachers or that they were earning only modest salaries, and they simply could not afford to make gifts. Then they were asked if they make annual donations to other organizations or causes; everyone said yes. Then came silence; then came laughter. Once the alumni realized that "poverty" was an excuse and not a reason, more useful information came to light: they do not see the school making a difference in the world or helping address problems in education that many of them deal with every day—so they see little reason to support it. This exercise was repeated with the same results at each of the subsequent focus groups.

The survey data provided quantitative corroboration. Almost all alumni from the School of Education (93 percent) said they give money *on a regular basis* to charities, cultural organizations, public interest groups, or other not-for-profit organizations. But 70 to 90 percent were not at all aware of five major programs the school had developed in recent years to help address some of the issues and problems they were most concerned about—perhaps because, as the survey also indicated, alumni received little substantive communication about the school and felt that the school magazine was mostly irrelevant to their interests.

The study of the School of Law alumni (four focus groups followed by a telephone survey of four hundred conducted in October 1995) produced similar findings. About a third of all law school alumni did not know enough about the school even to offer an opinion about whether or not it is a "leader among law schools," and almost 60 percent could not point to a single area of the law in which the school is preeminent. Though it is understandable that alumni may have limited awareness of recent changes and developments at the school, it is disturbing that so few of them recognized even the most fundamental qualities that distinguish the school. Again, the study also found that alumni were inadequately informed—and even confused—by the school's communications (which, like the School of Education's magazine, have since been redesigned).

Three focus groups followed by a telephone survey of 402 alumni from the School of Medicine were conducted in May 1996. The most interesting issue concerned the school's solicitation strategy. Each year, medical school alumni were being asked by the dean to give to the Stanford Medical Fund, while also being asked to support the school by making gifts to a fund created by the Medical Alumni Association (which were then given to the dean). This dual solicitation strategy might have made sense if alumni felt it provided them with meaningful alternatives in how to support the school, or if they trusted the Medical Alumni Association to spend the money more wisely than the dean. But the research indicated just the opposite. The dual solicitations were three times as likely to *confuse* alumni as they were to provide them with a meaningful choice in how to support the school. Alumni were almost twice as likely to trust the *dean* more than the Medical Alumni Association to spend the money where it has the greatest impact. The overwhelming majority (70 percent) did not feel they had more say in how their gifts were used by giving to the Medical Alumni Association.

It was therefore recommended that alumni receive only a single solicitation, that fundraising be left to the dean and his development staff, and that the Medical Alumni Association could best support the school by focusing directly on events and programs to increase alumni involvement.

As with the Schools of Education and Law, the study of graduate alumni from the School of Engineering (four focus groups followed by a telephone survey of six hundred conducted in July 1995) revealed that alumni were unaware of what the school is doing to deserve its reputation (and their support). One focus group participant likened the school to a Rube Goldberg contraption because "it has bells and whistles and all sorts of ingenious things going on, but I have little idea what the darn thing actually does."

Because the survey found that alumni were twice as likely to identify more closely with their department than with the school, it was recommended that The Engineering Fund abandon its school-based appeals in favor of department-based appeals. After the survey, a market test was conducted in which a randomly selected half of alumni from its largest departments received a school-based appeal, and the other half received a departmental appeal. Although the money was still raised for unrestricted use by the school's dean, the appeals from the department chairs outperformed the schoolwide appeal by a third, both in participation and in dollars raised. The following year, the entire direct appeal program for the School of Engineering adopted the departmental approach, and the fund achieved a 44 percent increase in participation and a 28 percent increase in dollars raised.

The study also found that the interests of engineering alumni are not limited to their individual fields, so a two-tiered communications strategy was recommended—schoolwide communications to keep alumni informed about the breadth of activity across all engineering departments (and to ensure that all alumni receive the same consistent messages), along with departmental newsletters to provide depth on a more targeted basis. Two years after certain departments established newsletters to complement the redesigned schoolwide communications, a follow-up survey was conducted to measure the effect of this strategy.

Conducted in July 1997 with 605 of the school's graduate alumni, the follow-up telephone survey indicated that the new communications program was working. Alumni who received the departmental newsletters were much more likely than those who did not receive the newsletters to feel like an important part of both the school and the department community and to feel better informed about faculty, current research, and alumni. They were also significantly more aware of various qualities of the school, and had more favorable perceptions on a variety of measures.

The follow-up survey also indicated that the time had come to seriously apply online technology to alumni relations and communications. As of July 1997, 88 percent of all engineering alumni said they used both e-mail and the Web—including virtually everyone (99 percent) under the age of forty, 95 percent of alumni in their forties, 88 percent of alumni in their fifties, and 62 percent of alumni sixty or older. Furthermore, in just two years, online usage had increased dramatically—by about twenty percentage points—among *all* age groups, not just among younger alumni. Indeed, by July 1997, e-mail and the Web had become regular parts of their lives, used as much by alumnae as alumni.

Online Services for Alumni

Although engineers may be the most likely of alumni to be online, other studies indicated that other alumni were not far behind. But to provide online services and resources that alumni will find meaningful and actually use, it is necessary to first understand the underlying *benefits* they want—and then design the features that best deliver those benefits. Therefore, six focus groups were conducted in November 1997 with alumni who use e-mail and the Web. As diverse as these alumni were (undergraduate, graduate, and dual degree holders, from their mid-twenties to early seventies), the underlying benefits they want from Stanford online are the same:

- Connectedness, or community—with other alumni and with the university (or their school or department)
- Awareness—of news and information about what is happening at the university, current research and scholarship, alumni association programs, and local alumni events
- Access to university resources—libraries, faculty and student research, health and medical resources
- Job and career networking
- Continuing education—more for personal enrichment than for professional development

Fortunately, the benefits alumni want from the university online coincide with the challenges the university most urgently needs to meet—demonstrating the positive impact it has on the world and why it deserves their support, making alumni feel part of the Stanford community, and becoming relevant to them once again.

The key to delivering online benefits to alumni is literally *to deliver* them. As often as participants in the focus groups use the Web, they were not visiting any Stanford sites frequently or on a regular basis. But they were eager for Stanford to employ e-mail subscription lists and other "push" techniques to deliver news, information, and items of interest directly to their attention. They most wanted to subscribe to lists that would inform them of

- News about the university as a whole, covering top stories as well as information about student life, curriculum, and current research
- Similar news and information specific to their school, department, or program
- New online services and resources available to alumni
- Alumni events and volunteer opportunities in their local area

Participants indicated three essential requirements for e-mail lists to be appealing. First, information must be sent frequently enough to be timely, but no more frequently than needed to keep readers current. The frequency of each list therefore depends on its subject matter. Second, each time a list is distributed, it must include clear instructions on how to "unsubscribe." Third, and perhaps most important, content must be brief. Ideally, each mailing would be little more than a series of headlines with hypertext links to the full stories.

Almost all the participants said they use the Web mostly to find specific information. They do not just surf; thus, they spend little time simply browsing around the Stanford sites. With this in mind, subscription lists can help increase awareness of the sites they link to and may induce alumni to bookmark those sites and visit them without being prompted.

In addition to enabling the university to reach large constituencies in a timely manner, subscription lists can also help engage and inform unique populations with focused interests (such as alumni living in Asia and fans of each of the major teams). They can also supplement direct mail marketing for groups with limited marketing budgets (such as alumni travel programs, the art museum, and the university symphony).

Every entity with an e-mail list should promote the list on its Web site. Alumni warned, however, that their limited browsing would leave them unaware of many lists unless those lists were also compiled in a single and conspicuous location.

Automated list servers can be used not only for one-way bulletins with news and information but also for discussion groups among alumni. Most participants agreed that e-mail discussion groups could, at least theoretically, help strengthen their connection and sense of community with other alumni. However, there was only lukewarm interest in subscribing to Stanford discussion groups, because many have found that broadly defined groups clutter their e-mail boxes with too much chatter on topics of little interest to them, whereas more narrowly focused groups often have too little traffic to be of much value. They also questioned whether Stanford discussion groups would significantly differ from groups already available online.

Like increased awareness and connectedness, greater access to university resources can help Stanford remain relevant to alumni and make them feel part of the Stanford community. The resource to which alumni most want online access is the libraries, but they also want access to various databases, faculty and student research, and work in the arts and humanities (including creative writing, music, art, and campus humor). Not surprisingly, older alumni very much want access to health and medical resources, and younger alumni want access to services for job and career networking. The latter, however, is also of interest to older alumni who are involved in recruiting and hiring for jobs and internships: they would like an inside track on Stanford's large and diverse talent pool.

Whereas the university can attract alumni to its Web sites by including features that deliver the underlying benefits they want, other features can help stimulate repeat visits. Some of these are "value-added" features that increase the utility of a site, some are simply fun, and some are both. Citing features that appear in many of the most successful commercial sites, alumni said they would be more likely to pay repeat visits to Stanford sites if the sites included free downloads, relevant links, and even factoids, polls, and contests. As one alumna remarked of polls and contests, "Okay, so they're the Internet equivalent of those love testers in barrooms that rate your sex appeal, but they do engage the visitor."

Alumni do *not* want advertisements on Stanford Web sites, nor do they want to be overwhelmed with offers to buy Stanford merchandise. (They do want to be able to purchase such merchandise online but suggested that all items for sale be included on a single site.) They especially do not want to be solicited for gifts by e-mail.

Regarding Stanford's existing Web sites, alumni felt first of all that the university home page impeded, rather than facilitated, access to the information they wanted—because it was cluttered with too many links that are irrelevant to their interests and because it was organized in a way that made little sense to them. Just about everyone was baffled or bemused that Stanford had chosen the color of its arch rival, the University of California–Berkeley, as the dominant visual element in its home page.

Because of the multitude and diversity of the university's Web sites, alumni recognized that Stanford faces an unusual challenge in making information and resources easy to find. This challenge was underscored as it became clear that many were unaware of a host of resources that were already available to them—mainly because much of the Stanford Web was organized from an internal or bureaucratic perspective, rather than from an audience perspective. Alumni further noted that navigation was hindered by a lack of coordination, unity, and consistent standards among the sites, which also gave some of them the impression that Stanford "is a place where no one talks to anyone else." It was also remarked that there was no consistent visual style among the many sites, and although most felt that the many styles reflect the diversity of character that makes Stanford special, they also noted that more could be done to brand the sites with a Stanford identity.

Finally, alumni felt that many of the sites and features they did find (such as the alumni locator and the alumni contact service) needed improved functionality to be of real value.

At the time this study was conducted, collecting alumni e-mail addresses was considered the most urgent priority for making Stanford's online services of significant value in alumni relations and communications. Therefore, in addition to advising that the issues discussed above be addressed, it was recommended that Stanford immediately take a number of actions to collect as many e-mail addresses as possible. Other recommendations included creating alumni advisory boards for online issues, finding a mechanism by which e-mail addresses can be shared among different Stanford databases, and establishing a high-level campuswide working group to facilitate greater unity and consistency among the many Stanford Web sites. The report also suggested that it may be necessary for each school to employ its own Web master in order to realize the full potential of the Internet and the Web. It is unrealistic to expect that existing staff has the time or expertise to adequately develop and maintain effective sites and online services. It is important to recognize, however, that the return on such an investment may be great in terms of a more informed, engaged, and supportive alumni community.

Research on Reports and Advertising

As online services are launched and promoted, market research will be able to measure their penetration and impact, just as research has been conducted to assess the readership and effectiveness of printed material. In December 1995, shortly after The Stanford Fund mailed its first annual report to alumni, a telephone survey was conducted with 402 undergraduate degree holders in order to gauge the readership of the report and measure how effectively it informed readers and communicated certain messages.

Sixty-two percent of alumni recalled receiving the report, and 59 percent of those who recalled it (or 37 percent of all alumni) said they looked at it. For the most part, however, alumni who looked at the report were no more aware than those who did not look at it of certain basic facts about The Stanford Fund that were included in the report.

Among all alumni who looked at the report, at least three-quarters said it helped give them a better sense that Stanford appreciates the gifts that alumni make; that alumni gifts do have an impact when added together; and that individual gifts, however modest, do make a difference. On the other hand, barely half said it helped them better understand how alumni gifts are used. This was particularly disappointing as it was one of the primary objectives of the report, which included an entire page with a chart illustrating how the funds are used. Other data from the survey suggested that this vital information may have simply been lost in the clutter of less essential text and tables.

A year later, another survey was conducted (with 602 undergraduate degree holders) to assess the effectiveness of the redesigned second annual report. The most notable measured difference between the two reports was that many more alumni recalled receiving the second one, perhaps because it was more distinguishable from other mail. (The first report was a small pamphlet mailed without an envelope, whereas the second report was a large spiral-bound piece sent in a Stanford envelope.)

In most other ways, however, response to the second report was almost identical with that to the first report. Although the second report was much more elaborate (and expensive) than the first report, the same percentage of alumni who recalled the report said they looked at it, and the same messages were and were not effectively communicated. Also as with the first report, those who looked at the second report were no more likely than those who did not look at it to know the most basic facts about The Stanford Fund. Once again, some of the most important information was buried under the mass of other information. Plans were made for the third annual report to take a different approach to displaying information.

Advertising campaigns can also be tested with research, and in June 1997, four focus groups were conducted with older alumni to gauge their response to a series of ads for the Office of Planned Giving that was to appear in *Stanford* magazine. The research convincingly demonstrated that the ads not only missed their intended target (rank-and-file alumni without great fortunes) but actually conveyed a message *opposite* to what was intended. Almost unanimously, alumni in the focus groups said that the ads implied that they themselves were not appropriate candidates for making a planned gift. Indeed, they felt that the ads actively *excluded* them by suggesting one must be wealthy to make a meaningful planned gift, by appealing to "the ego instead of the soul," and by emphasizing money rather than people—the gift rather than the beneficiaries of the gift.

This research demonstrates the importance of testing material and messages with their intended audiences—because "insiders" cannot always anticipate the perceptions and reactions of an external audience. The tested ads were scrapped.

Methodological Issues Unique to Research with Alumni

One of the most significant differences between research with alumni and research with the general public is that alumni are much more cooperative. Because cooperation seemed unusually high on the first few telephone surveys with Stanford alumni, a test survey was conducted to compare the cooperation rate—and detect any potential bias—on alumni surveys that do and do not identify Stanford as the sponsor. The test survey (conducted with four hundred undergraduate alumni in July 1995) did not identify Stanford as the sponsor, and no mention was ever made of Stanford; respondents were simply told that a public opinion research firm was conducting a brief survey on higher education. Although circumstances did not allow for a split-sample test, the results were compared with an almost identical (but sponsored) survey conducted at about the same time with a different sample from the same population.

The difference in cooperation was profound. Indeed, cooperation was five times higher on the survey that identified Stanford as the sponsor—one initial refusal for every 11.7 completed interviews, compared with one initial refusal for every 2.1 completed interviews on the anonymous survey. Similar high cooperation rates have been obtained not only on subsequent surveys with Stanford alumni but also on a comparative survey conducted later that year with Princeton, Yale, and the University of Pennsylvania alumni.

Although the university's sponsorship may lend legitimacy to a survey, it appears that the high cooperation may be due more to the respondents' affiliation with the university. In February 1998, a telephone survey about continuing education was conducted among 402 young adults in the Silicon Valley.

All respondents were told that the survey was being conducted by Stanford, but there were four times as many refusals per completed interview among nonalumni than among alumni.

The test survey was also conducted to see if identifying Stanford as the sponsor favorably biases alumni responses due to "social desirability." There was concern that alumni might be reluctant to offer unfavorable answers when Stanford addresses them by name and clearly knows other information about them as well. As it turns out, however, this concern is unfounded. On most measures, there was no difference whatsoever, but on one or two measures, alumni were just barely *more critical* when Stanford was identified as the sponsor than when it was not. Three possible explanations come to mind:

Alumni may perceive a sponsored survey as an opportunity to express criticism that will actually be heard and maybe make a difference.

Alumni may be reluctant to criticize their alma mater to outsiders, not wishing to air its dirty laundry in public. They may feel that expressions of dissatisfaction are best kept "in the family."

The frame of reference may be different. In an anonymous survey, alumni may consider their responses in context of many other (less prestigious) institutions, whereas in a sponsored survey, they may consider their responses in context of Stanford alone or in context of its peer institutions. For instance, some respondents may feel that compared with the education they could have received at XYZ University, they are very satisfied with their experiences at Stanford. On the other hand, compared with what they *expected* from Stanford (or think they could have gotten at Harvard), they are only somewhat satisfied.

The test survey reassured us that we could—and should—continue to identify Stanford in most future alumni surveys. Potential bias appears to be small, and cost savings from higher cooperation rates are large. Moreover, any bias that may be introduced seems to be *unfavorable* to the university, so the data are unlikely to mislead us into a false sense of security (which could cause much more mischief than data that might throw an extra ray of light on certain weaknesses).

Because response rates are so high with alumni on telephone surveys—and often so low on self-administered mail surveys—it is highly advisable to survey alumni by telephone whenever appropriate. (Examining when each of the different survey methodologies is most appropriate is beyond the scope of this chapter, but an excellent discussion of this and many other issues about conducting survey research can be found in *Mail and Telephone Surveys: The Total Design Method* by Don A. Dillman, published by Wiley.) In phone surveys of alumni, nonresponse bias is minimized; in mail surveys, it is usually a significant threat to statistical validity and reliability. Phone surveys also take much less time to complete (days instead of weeks or months), eliminate the administrative burden of mailing two or three waves of reminders to nonrespondents, and (depending on the sample size) can ultimately be less expensive to conduct. Furthermore, the introduction of computer-assisted telephone interviewing technology (known as CATI) about ten years ago has made telephone surveys preferable for a host of methodological reasons too numerous to discuss in this chapter. All of this may change, of course, as Web usage becomes universal.

Just as alumni are very cooperative on telephone surveys, so too are they cooperative in focus groups, which they especially appreciate because the discussion format allows them the opportunity to offer their opinions in depth. Recruiting alumni for focus groups is remarkably easy, and no incentive fees are necessary—not even for lawyers or doctors, who often command hundreds of dollars apiece to participate in commercial focus groups.

Not surprisingly, alumni are also more likely than the general public to show up for the focus groups they say they will attend. Although it is still necessary to follow the initial recruitment with a confirmation letter and a reminder call, care must be taken so that *too many* alumni do not attend. Consumer focus groups typically recruit fourteen people per group, hoping that eight to ten will show up. If too many arrive, some are simply paid their incentive, thanked, and sent home. Few people object to this: they usually have no idea who is sponsoring the research and are happy to take the money and run. This cannot be done with alumni, who come not for money but to give their opinions and be heard. They get very offended if the university asks for their thoughts and then, after they arrive, they are told that their opinions are not needed after all. To reduce the risk of running a group with an unwieldy number of participants, I recruit only twelve alumni per group. Unforeseen circumstances often prevent a few from attending, but if all twelve do show up, I squeeze them all in. (The second time all twelve alumni showed up, I tried to finesse the situation by inviting two of them to share the "client's" perspective by watching from the observation room with the Stanford staff. Suffice it to say that this was *not* acceptable to them and was never attempted again.)

Focus groups with alumni require greater sensitivity in other ways as well. To begin with, the invitation must be more forthcoming about the topic than it is with many other groups. This is no problem when the groups are designed to explore general topics, such as their relationship with the university, their feelings about it, and their major concerns. But the more specific the topic, the more thorny this issue can be, because alumni with little interest in the topic or with negative feelings about it—who may well be the ones you most want to hear from—will opt out and not accept the invitation if it is too specific. On the other hand, if the invitation is too vague about the topic, some alumni feel duped or deceived and can become disruptive (another lesson learned the hard way). A very delicate balance must therefore be attained when recruiting for many alumni groups.

Regardless of the topic or how clearly it is stated, some alumni come to focus groups with agendas of their own, dead set on airing certain grievances and pet peeves even if they have nothing whatsoever to do with the issues being explored. Although this can happen at any time, one should be especially cautious about—or avoid—conducting groups shortly after the admissions office sends out its acceptance and rejection letters.

Student callers can be used for focus group invitations, but they are inappropriate to conduct surveys unless they are trained and supervised by a survey lab. Using the same students who make fundraising calls to conduct surveys is especially inappropriate, because they are trained to express enthusiasm for the university, answer questions, offer their own thoughts, and vary each call according to the prospect on the line (all of which is anathema to proper survey interviewing. Survey interviews must be unbiased by the interviewer's feelings and expressions, noninterpretive, and free from variation).

Another issue to be aware of when calling alumni is that most of them have full-time jobs and seldom arrive home by 5:00 P.M., which is when interviewing usually begins for surveys with the general public. To avoid wasting time and money reaching answering machines—and to avoid overrepresentation of older and retired alumni, who are more likely to be at home at that hour—it is advisable to start calling at 6:30 or 7:00 P.M. Although this leaves fewer calling hours in each evening, they are much more productive and cost-efficient hours.

An even more efficient way to invite alumni to focus groups (if the population is right and if you have the addresses) is to do it by e-mail. One person can quickly fill two focus groups—at no cost whatsoever—simply by sending the invitation to a list of alumni e-mail addresses. Recruiting the same two groups by phone can take twenty person-hours if students make the calls (or can cost a fortune if done professionally). Focus group facilities and interviewing firms charge from $65 to $100 for *each person they recruit,* which is expensive when recruiting for four groups (forty-eight people) and outrageous when recruiting for six groups (seventy-two people).

I have attempted in this chapter to illustrate the range of alumni issues for which market research can provide useful and actionable information. In closing, it may be helpful to explain why having an in-house researcher is more cost-effective than contracting with a research firm (if more than an occasional study is conducted). Like auto repair, market research involves expenses for parts and labor, and as at a garage or car dealership, labor is much more expensive than parts. A telephone survey that incurs $4,000 in hard costs for interviewing (parts) may cost anywhere from $15,000 to $25,000 if contracted out to a research firm, which is billing for its time and expertise in designing and managing the study, writing the instrument, preparing the sample, analyzing the data, and writing a report (labor). Likewise, a pair of focus groups conducted by a research firm may cost from $8,000 to $20,000 (prices vary widely for qualitative research), although the hard cost of renting the facility, complete with catering, is only about $1,000. Clearly, the more of each study that an in-house researcher can do, the more cost-effective the position can be. If the in-house researcher has experience conducting, analyzing, and reporting both quantitative and qualitative research (if he or she can crunch numbers as well as moderate focus groups), your budget will need to cover only the hard costs and the researcher's salary.

The resources required for in-house research are minimal. Apart from employing an administrative assistant (shared with someone else), I am a one-man shop with no staff, and I have been able to complete eight or nine studies each year. Given the high cooperation rate, my interviewing costs for an eight- or nine-minute telephone survey of four hundred alumni are usually about $3,000. Obviously, a twenty-minute survey of six hundred alumni would cost more. Quality and cost vary among interviewing firms. Some of the factors that determine interviewing costs are the length of the survey, the sample size, the number of invalid phone numbers dialed, the number of attempts needed to reach respondents, the cooperation rate, and the number of open-ended questions (which take time to record and then code). Besides standard office software, the only computer resources needed are a graphics-and-charting program, a database, and a statistical analysis package. A crystal ball can be helpful, however, and a direct phone line to the caves of Delphi is also reassuring.

More information about the alumni research conducted at Stanford and a bibliography for survey and focus group research can be found on my Web site: http://www.stanford.edu/~jpearson/

JEROLD PEARSON is director of market research at Stanford University's Office of Development.

Both routine monitoring reports and special studies contribute to effective fundraising efforts and the provision of services to alumni at the Massachusetts Institute of Technology.

Planning and Evaluating Massachusetts Institute of Technology Alumni Services and Fundraising

Joseph S. Collins, William J. Hecht, Diana Tilley Strange

Alumni offices usually focus their attention on two generally agreed-on operating principles—serving their alumni with programs and services of the highest quality and meeting institutional needs. The mission of the Association of Alumni and Alumnae of the Massachusetts Institute of Technology (MIT) is just that—serving the needs of our alumni for lifelong relationships with one another and with the Institute and serving MIT's needs for alumni support and involvement. This chapter illustrates the important role that research data have played, as we have striven to fulfill this mission with a commitment to the principle of continual improvement.

In the first part of this chapter, we examine our recent long-range, strategic-planning experience and the value gained from using survey results to set alumni relations priorities. In the second part, we look back at the alumni fund in the 1980s, examine the usefulness of research in turning a moribund annual fund into one that has shown continual growth over nearly twenty years, and demonstrate the value of these research tools in monitoring results against annual goals. In both these cases, another defining element of the MIT Alumni Association becomes apparent—the vital role that alumni volunteers play in contributing to the dynamic nature of our alumni programs.

It is important to clarify the MIT context. At MIT, we pride ourselves on being unique; perhaps the MIT Alumni Association's relationship to the Institute is not unique among college alumni organizations, but it is not common. The alumni association reports not to the president of MIT but to a volunteer board of directors selected by an elected alumni National Selection Committee

(NSC). The NSC also selects fifteen members of the MIT Corporation (MIT's board of trustees) and many members of the corporation's visiting committees. In addition, the president of the alumni association serves by virtue of office on the corporation. This alumni governance role at MIT is well grounded in MIT's history.

The association is the home of the MIT Alumni Fund, our annual fund, which reported in excess of $28,700,000 in gifts to MIT in fiscal year 1998. Our alumni activities program is typical, including at the core strong class reunions and regional programs (clubs and so forth). In addition, the association publishes *Technology Review*, MIT's magazine of innovation, the alumni magazine that has a growing national subscriber base as large as its alumni circulation. The association is responsible for the alumni records database, including gift records.

Even though we are legally an independent alumni organization, the sole source of association funding is MIT's operating budget, reflecting the high value to MIT of the association's work on behalf of the Institute. To implement alumni services and programs and to support MIT's needs, the MIT Alumni Association depends on a partnership between an experienced professional staff and the more than four thousand alumni volunteers who actively serve MIT every year.

Establishing Long-Range Alumni Relations Priorities

Periodically, the MIT Alumni Association's board of directors initiates a long-range planning process in which we assess alumni needs for services from the association and the Institute and examine whether the association is meeting those needs. During the academic years 1994 and 1995, a Long-Range Strategy Committee (LRSC) was appointed by the board to take a fresh look at the work of the association. The LRSC engaged an outside market research firm to test the perceived needs and reactions of alumni both for services we were offering and others being offered by peer institutions. This section discusses the issues raised by the long-range planning committee, presents the research questions and results, and describes the ways the data have helped shape both new and ongoing programs in the past three to four years.

In the summer of 1992, MIT had completed a successful capital campaign during which much of the association's energy and resources were focused on fundraising objectives. To answer the question about the postcampaign focus, the board decided to examine the whole of the association's programs and activities, even raising questions about such successful activities as the alumni fund and challenging the appropriateness of supporting a national magazine. An ad hoc board committee in the late 1980s, before the end of the campaign, had conducted an informal study, which compared MIT association services for alumni with those of similar institutions. This committee asked if we really were offering the services our alumni needed and wanted. The board seemed to be suggesting that perhaps we needed some radical changes.

Long-Range Strategy Committee Planning Process. When the LRSC was formed, its purpose was described this way: "It has been more than a decade since a fresh look has been given to the strategy and direction of the Alumni Association. Since that time, significant change has taken place in the nature and composition of individuals comprising the Association's membership. . . . The fundamental purpose of the effort [is] to answer questions about whether the Association is responsive to the needs of its constituents and, as necessary, implement appropriate changes."

The effort was undertaken with a team that comprised seven alumni volunteers, five MIT staff, and one alumnus on the faculty. The committee was to report to the board with recommendations for action. Separate working groups were convened to address each of four planning questions (or sets of questions), with each group establishing its own methodology by gathering historical materials, benchmarking, and conducting research. The four areas of inquiry were

1. What is the mission of the association, and what are its supporting objectives?
2. Is there duplication or are there gaps in fundraising activities between the Institute development office and the association's alumni fund? Would an alternative structure help realize greater efficiency and effectiveness?
3. Are the association's communications and publications effective? Is the value of the alumni magazine commensurate with its cost?
4. How do alumni view and evaluate association services? What services not being provided should be? Are there services that should be reduced or eliminated? How effective are existing "business services," and are they in line with the association mission and alumni needs?

This chapter reports on the LRSC investigation of the fourth set of questions, undertaken in the context of this broader investigation of the roles and responsibilities for the association. The model outlined below may be helpful to the reader who wishes to investigate similar questions.

Evaluating Alumni Services. The alumni services subcommittee of the LRSC established its committee objectives:

- To evaluate how MIT's alumni services are perceived by alumni as compared with other universities
- To analyze and reach conclusions on prospective changes to services, such as adding new services and changing emphasis on current services, including reduction or elimination of some services
- To propose a plan for action

Early on, this working group determined that professional, quality market research would be required to evaluate its questions about current services and the advisability of new services. MIT was in a retrenchment mode; across the Institute, services and programs were being evaluated for efficiency and effectiveness. The Institute was in the throes of a reengineering process, which had been inspired by a popular book written by two alumni, *Reengineering the Corporation*. Any proposal to initiate programs would need to be accompanied by a plan for reallocating resources and probably generating additional resources outside MIT. Especially in such a context, it was agreed that only an outside consultant could provide the objectivity needed to take such a hard look at well-established programs, the results of which might lead to recommendations for radical change. The committee reported that it would need to rely on "professional knowledge for developing meaningful results."

The Survey. Two members of the committee interviewed a number of consulting firms nationwide and reported a fundamental difference in the proposed consulting approaches—telephone versus direct mail questionnaires. The committee selected Sibley Associates, a firm located north of Boston, which had recommended a phone survey. In selecting Sibley, the committee cited "experience with university surveys, the ability to probe and gain insight from the respondent and value compared with cost" as factors that weighed in over the "percent accuracy loss of the telephone survey (approximately 95 percent versus 97.5 percent for a questionnaire)." Also, the results could be made available almost immediately because the questionnaire would be computerized, and answers would be keyed in as the interviews were conducted.

To develop the questionnaire, Sibley interviewed key staff leaders to understand the purpose of the survey. He sought input from volunteers as well as from the entire association staff on what kinds of questions should be asked. With a laundry list of association current activities as well as potential alumni services offered by other alumni groups, the consultant developed an eleven-question survey to which some additional demographic questions were appended.

The questions were designed to give us the ability to compare MIT with other schools as well as to compare appropriateness, usefulness, and likelihood of use on a set of seventeen types of services. The intent of the survey was to gather generalized information. If more detail was desired, new surveys might be required. (We did decide later to conduct a more comprehensive survey to understand alumni attitudes about the magazine.) The interview would consist of both closed and open-ended questions; each phone conversation would take about twelve minutes.

In the sample, the committee had asked particularly for representation of graduate-only alumni, recently graduated alumni, and women; the sample was selected to produce meaningful results for each set of alumni. The consultant would report that he completed 252 interviews with "a generally representative sample of MIT's alumni population." A supplemental subcell of fifty alumnae was included in the total number of interviews to ensure adequate coverage of women graduates.

Survey Results. The first question posed by the committee was: How is the MIT Alumni Association doing in comparison with other institutions? At the outset of the telephone interview, interviewers said only that they were calling for a major university with some questions about alumni activities and did not identify the client as MIT. The individual was asked to identify universities from which they had degrees and then was asked to compare alumni associations among those institutions.

According to the Sibley report, "Across the board, MIT alumni services outperforms the collected scoring for other alumni associations." This result, documented in Figure 2.1, was gratifying. Even so, it did turn up areas for attention, in particular the rating on "being responsive to alumni requests," a customer service issue. These data, in which MIT's showing is so strong, might well have been viewed with suspicion had we not used a reputable, experienced, outside research firm.

The second research objective was to determine alumni attitudes about current services, services being developed, and services under consideration. The seventeen services selected for evaluation were rated by alumni for appropriateness, usefulness, and the likelihood that they might use the service.

Each rating was interesting, but we were especially interested in the likelihood that alumni might actually use either current or developing services. We grouped the seventeen services according to whether or not they were "fully developed" programs, "currently being developed" programs, and "new opportunities." The fully developed set of alumni programs—for example, the magazine, reunions, and the travel program—were considered highly appropriate and very useful, with the likelihood of use ranging from a high of 89 percent for the magazine (much higher than those who actually get the magazine) to a low of 35 percent for the travel program, which reflects the much smaller number of alumni who actually choose to travel with MIT.

The programs currently being developed included alumni directories, with the highest rating for likelihood of use (79 percent), and on the lower side, celebrations for special groups, such as departments, living groups, and the like, which were at 36 percent. These data are consistent with our experience.

Finally, alumni reported that the likelihood of using the possible new opportunities is highest for services with MIT intellectual content, especially when delivered using electronic technologies. Figure 2.2 shows the top ten services ranked by likelihood of use.

Looking at the data overall, Sibley reported a list of six services that scored "strongly in all three dimensions (appropriateness, usefulness, and likelihood of use)." It is noteworthy that there is content in each that only MIT can provide. The six services are the alumni magazine; alumni registers and directories; access to MIT lectures, seminars, and faculty; sales of university intellectual material; use of computers and electronic technology for MIT services; and class reunions.

The lessons learned from the survey can be summed up in five statements, which became the guiding principles for the recommendations of the LRSC and subsequently for the implementation of those recommendations:

• The association's major ongoing programs are solid and effective.
• An alumni magazine is the most highly valued MIT alumni service.

Figure 2.1. Rating of the MIT Alumni Association Programs and Services

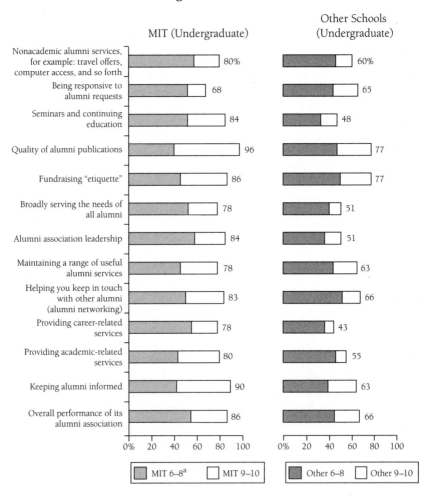

^aRating scale: 1 = poor to 10 = excellent

Source: MIT Alumni/ae Services Study, Feb. 1994

**Figure 2.2. Likelihood of Use of Top Ten
MIT Alumni Association Programs**

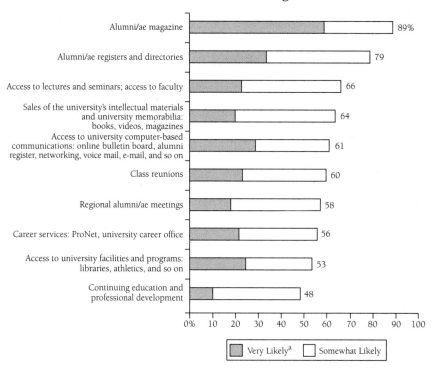

ᵃLikelihood of use ranged on a five-point scale from not at all likely to very likely.
Source: MIT Alumni/ae Services Study, Feb. 1994

- The service most in demand is directory services; alumni want to know how to find one another.
- Services most important to alumni are those that have content that only MIT can offer.
- Service development opportunities include online services, career and professional development, and lifelong learning opportunities.

New Areas for Service. The committee concluded that the association should continue to investigate avenues for "assisting career and professional development." We should begin development and testing to deliver services via electronic technologies. They said we are emphasizing many of the right "as-is" services, but we need continually to address the appropriateness and effectiveness of them—for example, developing more delivery options for directory information and expanding what might be termed "lifelong learning" activities. They recommended that we approach with caution the pursuit of services such as credit cards, group insurance, and discount programs.

Impact of Survey Results. The LRSC presented its recommendations to the association board of directors in the fall of 1994, including the recommendations for new and expanded services described above. In the four years since the report, the association has been working to implement these recommendations, beginning with a major reallocation of staff and budget resources. Three experienced senior staff members were freed up to investigate computer-based service opportunities, to work on career and professional support services, and to develop a more robust lifelong learning program.

Alumni network services on the Internet. The board-appointed planning committee proposed a new World Wide Web Alumni Network Services (ANS) program, for MIT alumni only, to include an identification and authentication procedure associated with a permanent MIT e-mail address and an e-mail routing service. Services to follow included an online alumni directory; bulletin board; and conferencing services, providing links among alumni, current MIT students, and MIT faculty.

In the first eighteen months, over fifteen thousand users registered; 70 percent of the class of 1997 use the service; nearly four hundred thousand messages were forwarded during the first five weeks of 1998 (an average of ten thousand messages a day). Reallocated resources include three full-time staff members and $100,000 in program budget. In fiscal year 1999, for the first time, substantial new Institute resources have been allocated to ANS.

Career and professional services. The Institute Career Assistance Network was launched in fall 1996, with two thousand alumni mentors having responded to nearly one thousand requests since the program began. A cross-functional staff working group was assigned to coordinate expanding professional support activities, including Web-based offerings. Partnerships with other MIT offices and departments are under development.

New lifelong learning opportunities for alumni. The MIT on the Road program began offering seminars in Florida, New York, Chicago, and Lisbon in 1998, and plans exist for expansion in 1999. Alumni conferences have been held in Switzerland and in Lisbon.

On the Web, services with MIT libraries and courses offered jointly with MIT Center for Advanced Educational Services and other departments are under investigation.

Directory services. A Web-based online directory has been established, including capacity for alumni to update personal records. Minidirectories are now available for club regions and special-interest groups.

Though the staff reallocation to allow the initiatives described above did have the unanticipated outcome of strengthening class and geographic programs, most attention has been focused on new opportunities. The impact of asking several of our most senior staff members to do some new things was to give increased opportunities to some of our other experienced staff members. They have risen to the challenge with significant improvements in the basic alumni services we have provided all along. Even so, we believe we could be using the results of this research to greater value in improving and sustaining our core business.

Over the past three years, we have used these results well with key alumni volunteers and other Institute offices, but we could still make more use of the data with our own staff. A recently convened staff strategy group charged with investigating an issue for the association board has been reexamining the survey results and taking a fresh look at the recommendations of the LRSC. So the research continues to have an impact on today's planning as well.

Finally, this research has been very important to current discussions with MIT about new resources required to continue the development of these new programs; it has demonstrated to the MIT central administration that the association has taken an unvarnished look at itself. The outcomes have been impressive, and the future will require continued assessment and evaluation.

Setting Fundraising Goals and Evaluating Results

It will come as no surprise that at MIT, judicious use of research based on extensive analysis of alumni data collected over many decades forms the basis for decision making in our annual fund. We have the benefit of data-rich alumni records, which have been analyzed over many years to help set annual and five-year fund goals, to inform capital campaign planning, and to justify resource allocations.

The alumni association at MIT has been responsible for the solicitation of the alumni fund from its inception more than fifty years ago. The alumni fund board, composed of alumni volunteers appointed by the association board of directors, is responsible for setting goals for the annual fund, establishing crediting rules and donor recognition policies, and authorizing special fundraising initiatives designed to meet particular goals.

Many annual funds report only unrestricted current use gifts, but at MIT, gifts reported in the alumni fund are a record of all alumni giving over the fiscal year, cash only. We report the first $100,000 of every gift for any purpose made by any alumnus or alumna received during the crediting period, including capital gifts and deferred gifts. Alumni fund totals also include corporate matching gifts as well as gifts from nonalumni parents and other friends of the Institute. The reader should keep these "house rules" in mind.

In 1980, the MIT annual fund reported $5,000,000 in total gifts from twenty thousand donors; in 1998, the fund results were in excess of $27,000,000 with nearly thirty-one thousand donors. This growth—over little more than fifteen years—was produced by a thoughtful, conscious process of feedback through sophisticated analysis of giving patterns, which has resulted in data that have informed long-term as well as short-term plans. In this section, we examine three particular situations in which this research has helped MIT understand the "behavior" of the annual fund and its contributors.

The current annual goal-setting methodology was first put in place in 1980, when the alumni fund board established a set of measurements by which to monitor fund results and assist in setting goals. First, we shall describe these data and how they have been collected and used.

In 1988, the alumni association board of directors mandated an integration of the annual fund and alumni relations staffs, providing more effective and efficient support for volunteers. The integration of these staff functions is a hallmark of the staffing structure in the MIT Alumni Association. The next section will describe research initiated at that time that demonstrates the tightly connected relationship between alumni relations activities and fundraising results.

Finally, we shall present a case study of a capital campaign initiative in which research data supported both the development and monitoring of the program. Implemented during MIT's last capital campaign (1987–1992), this nationwide annual fund program of personal solicitation involved more than five hundred volunteers and raised nearly $5,000,000 in annual gifts credited to the campaign.

These three illustrations document the usefulness of different kinds of research approaches. The first draws on a set of routine measurements designed to learn about the "anatomy" of our annual fund, which came to be used to monitor results. These measurements have been used for nearly twenty years and have become the bedrock for our annual and long-term goal setting. They are now so familiar that we almost forget they constituted "research" when we started out. The second illustrates research inspired by an organizational question that was raised when the alumni relations and annual fund staffs were melded together—for example, could we gain a better understanding of the common wisdom that good alumni relations and effective fundraising are structurally related? In this instance, the research process tested several sets of assumptions against the data. Finally, the case study shows the usefulness of data in developing and measuring a particular campaign-related annual fund initiative.

Setting Goals and Monitoring Results. In the 1970s, as a consequence of the tumultuous decade of the 1960s, annual giving at MIT experienced a stagnation of donors and a decline in percentage participation. As the decade wore on, members of the MIT Alumni Fund board expressed concern and began to search for rational explanations by seeking answers to several questions:

Was there a difference in the participation rate of undergraduate alumni as compared with those whose first degree was at the graduate level?
How many of those who gave in the prior year (LYBUNTS, "last year but not this") repeated in the following year?
What are the appropriate goals and measurements for the alumni fund beyond the obvious dollars and number of donors?

As the volunteers were asking these questions, there was a turnover in the staff leadership of the alumni fund; the new director undertook the task of formulating appropriate long-term (five-year) and short-term (one-year) alumni fund goals. For annual participation goals, the seven-year donor history (fiscal years 1975–1981) offered a useful perspective in two ways: by degree types—for example, undergraduate degree holders (UG) and graduate degree only (GSE); and by participation types—for example, repeat donors, sometime donors, and first-time donors.

Examination of the data in Table 2.1, along with other data we had collected, revealed

The living alumni base was growing at a rate in excess of one thousand per year, with graduate-level numbers (GSEs) increasing at a much faster clip than undergraduate numbers (UGs). This trend had been going on for many years.

Percentage participation for both UGs and GSEs varied over time—UGs between 40 and 50 percent (the 50 percent was achieved in 1972, not shown here) and GSEs in a much narrower band (28 to 32 percent).

Table 2.1. MIT Alumni Fund Actual Participation for Fiscal Years 1975–1981 and Goal for Fiscal Year 1982

Fund Year		Alumni Base	Participation Level (%)	A	+	B	+	C	=	Total Donors
FY75	U	34,445	45%							
	G	18,297	32	(78%)		(15%)				
	T	52,742	41	17,002	+	3,267	+	1,181	=	21,450
FY76	U	34,934	44							
	G	18,904	32	(80%)		(15%)				
	T	53,838	40	17,199	+	3,093	+	1,192	=	21,484
FY77	U	35,406	42							
	G	19,602	30	(77%)		(18%)				
	T	55,008	38	16,588	+	3,772	+	765	=	21,125
FY78	U	35,810	41							
	G	20,461	28	(77%)		(16%)				
	T	56,271	37	16,188	+	3,297	+	1,358	=	20,843
FY79	U	36,345	42							
	G	21,529	29	(80%)		(20%)				
	T	57,874	38	16,657	+	4,203	+	896	=	21,756
FY80	U	36,827	45							
	G	22,081	31	(82%)		(19%)				
	T	58,908	40	17,641	+	4,549	+	1,397	=	23,587
FY81	U	37,232	47							
	G	22,423	31	(80%)		(16%)				
	T	59,655	41	18,781	+	3,970	+	1,893	=	24,644
FY82	U									
	G			(80%)		(16%)				
	T	~60,500	41.6	19,700	+	3,950	+	1,550	=	25,200

Note: U = undergraduate, G = graduate student only, T = total

A = donors who also gave in prior year (LYBUNT conversion rate); B = donors who also gave at least once but not last year (SYBUNT conversion rate); C = first-time donors

Annual growth in total donors was greatly dependent on repeat donors (LYBUNTS). A conversion rate of 80 percent or greater usually ensures an increased number of donors overall.

Sometime donors (SYBUNTS, "some year but not this") had a pattern in which percentage conversion decreases significantly the further one moves from the year of the last gift (see discussion below).

First-time donors were an important component of this equation, especially gifts from alumni who had graduated in the five most recent years.

Using these data, a goal that increased donors by over 500 was set for fiscal year 1982, assuming a LYBUNT conversion of 80 percent (19,700), a cumulative SYBUNT conversion of nearly 4,000 donors, and 1,550 new donors. The longer-term participation goals centered on a "net" annual donor growth rate of 500 alumni per year in the period fiscal years 1980–1984. This led to a tactical shift in solicitation programs, spending more resources on phone solicitation, less on direct mail, and more effort aimed at recent graduates through a young alumni program and at GSE alumni through activities directed at links with the department in which they received their advanced degrees. Indeed, actual five-year results (fiscal years 1980–1984) yielded a net annual growth of more than 1,000 donors compared to the goal of 500 donors.

One important means of monitoring donor results in any given year is shown in Table 2.2. This table illustrates the conversion rates during fiscal year 1995 of donors by the year of their last gift. For example, the LYBUNTS (alumni who had given in fiscal year 1994) had a conversion rate of 79 percent. Those SYBUNTS whose last gift was in fiscal year 1993 had a conversion rate of 53 percent. The conversion rate dropped in relation to the year of one's last prior gift, such that five-year SYBUNTS (those with a last gift date of 1990) converted at a 16 percent rate. For those whose last gift was more than five years prior, the overall conversion rate shrinks to 5 percent. Based on these data, which are consistent year to year, we reduced significantly the resources expended to solicit greater than five-year SYBUNTS through direct mail and telephone. Further, a survey of alumni who had not made a gift in five years or more revealed that 70 percent of these alumni were unlikely ever again to make a gift, for reasons of disinterest in supporting MIT. However, the other 30 percent claimed that temporary considerations, including loss of job or unusually high expenses, were the reasons for their not having made a gift. Thus, we never stop entirely our efforts to solicit support from this cadre of alumni.

One especially intriguing piece of data tracked the pattern of giving, based on twenty-four different criteria, comparing GSE alumni and their UG counterparts. The MIT Alumni Fund Donor Profile Study, a probabalistic analysis, was first prepared in 1971 and was updated in 1981. The methodology measured donors with consecutive years of giving compared with occasional donors. The concept was to determine the likelihood of a gift in any given fund year. For GSE alumni who had given in several consecutive years, the data showed that, without regard to dollar amount, the probability of GSE giving

Table 2.2. Fiscal Year 1995 Contributor History Report

Donor Category Year of Last Gift	LYBUNTS 1994	SYBUNTS 1993	SYBUNTS 1992	SYBUNTS 1991	SYBUNTS 1990	SYBUNTS Before 1990	First-Time 1995	Total FY95 Contributors
7/18/94 BASE	28,139	5,560	2,905	2,192	1,754	17,357	0	
7/11/95	22,204	2,924	806	407	286	881	2,266	29,774
Percentage of Base	79	53	28	19	16	5		106[a]

Note: The second row distributes the 57,907 living alumni who were ever donors at the start of fiscal year 1995 (7/18/94) according to when they made their last gift. The third row distributes fiscal year 1995 donors by the year of the last gift and calculates a "conversion" rate.

[a]The 106 percent total represents the increase in donors from the fiscal year 1994 base total of 28,139.

in the next year is the same as for the UGs. Thus, with the graduate alumni base growing at a faster rate than the undergraduate base, one key to success in increasing total donors is to increase the number of first-time gifts from GSEs to MIT and then work hard to make them habitual annual donors.

Goal Setting in the Late 1990s. After more than fifteen years of data collection, the keys to increasing "net" donors continue to be LYBUNT conversion (80 percent target), some number of SYBUNTS (~5,000), and a strong number of first-time gifts (~1,500). With this rule of thumb in mind, we were surprised and concerned by results in the early 1990s. After increasing the donor number to 29,000 in fiscal year 1989, a capital fundraising campaign (fiscal years 1988–1992) with a gift-upgrading challenge fund led to stagnation of donors at 28,000. The first year postcampaign (fiscal year 1993) saw a drop to 27,000, with UG participation dropping to 40 percent and GSE to 28 percent. Key factors were the LYBUNT conversion rate of 77 percent, only 4,378 SYBUNT gifts, and a very low 1,037 first-time gifts. Through a special telethon effort launched in fiscal year 1994, alumni donors to the fund increased sharply to 30,577 by fiscal year 1997; LYBUNT conversion was back up to 79 percent; there were 5,086 SYBUNT gifts; and first-time donors approached the "magic" 1,500 total.

In a similar way, our efforts to upgrade support from regular donors rely on data tracked from prior years. From fiscal year 1980, when the median and modal gifts were $25, the fund doubled and redoubled that figure, achieving a $100 median in fiscal year 1993. At that point, goals were shifted to the number and percentage of donors giving at $500 plus, $2,000 plus, and $5,000 plus, with appropriate minimum donor recognition levels established at these key dollar thresholds.

To establish new five-year upgrading goals for the period fiscal years 1998–2002, the volunteer goals committee and fund staff analyzed the giving data in the prior five years (fiscal years 1992–1997). At each upgrading "target," the staff has specific new fundraising initiatives set forth to achieve these goals. Thus, in setting five-year goals, we look backward over a similar period to account for "bad" as well as "good" fund years to ensure that goals are realistic with appropriate tactics planned to achieve these objectives. In addition, independent of these long-term objectives, each year, the goals committee and staff propose one-year goals for the approval of the alumni fund board.

Monitoring and Measuring Results Today. Once the goals are set for an individual fund year, there are a variety of methods used to track results on a weekly and quarterly basis. Goals and results for fiscal year 1998 through December 31, 1997 are shown in Table 2.3, our quarterly reporting format for monitoring results.

The key report, MIT Alumni/ae Fund Weekly Progress Report (Table 2.4), tracks three-year weekly comparisons, in a variety of measures—overall participation by alumni donors only; participation by donor type (LYBUNTS, SYBUNTS, and first-time donors); donors at targeted gift levels; total alumni dollars; total dollars in fund (includes friends, nonalumni parents, and corporate matching gifts).

Table 2.3. Fiscal Year 1998 MIT Alumni Fund
Goals Measurements Report

Criteria	FY97 Results	Difference Between FY97 Results and FY98 Goals	FY98 Goals	Target 1/1/98	FY98 Results through 12/31/97	FY98 Change from FY97
Total Alumni Fund	$26.6M	+$900K	$27.5M	$16.5M	$16.4M	+$534K
Undergraduate						
Number donors to fund	19,576	+224	19,800	12,150	11,915	+311
Number donors ≥ $500	2,920	+180	3,100	1,950	1,916	+134
Percentage donors ≥ $500	14.9%	+.8%	15.7%	16%	16.1%	+.7%
Number first-time donors	750	50	800	425	428	+107
GSE						
Number donors to fund	11,001	+199	11,200	6,850	7,370	+489
Number donors ≥ $500	919	+81	1,000	625	683	+65
Percentage donors ≥ $500	8.4%	+.5%	8.9%	9.1%	9.3%	+.3%
Number first-time donors	688	+62	750	425	445	+68
Total						
Number donors to fund	30,577	+423	31,000	19,000	19,285	+800
Number first-time donors	1,438	+112	1,550	850	873	+175
Total Giving ≥ $2K						
Number donors ≥ $2K	1,080	+120	1,200	750	724	+63
Percentage donors ≥ $2K	3.5%	+.4%	3.9%	3.9%	3.8%	+.2%
Parents' Fund						
Total dollars	$378K	+$22K	$400K	$300K	$110K	−$164K
Number donors	568	+32	600	420	432	+42

Used to alert managers for tactical adjustments, this report is distributed electronically to staff every week, and quarterly to members of the MIT Alumni Fund board. Progress to date is discussed at the three meetings of the alumni fund board held in September, February, and June. In addition to the overall fund results, there are weekly donor and dollar comparison reports for both UGs and GSEs. Finally, each year the five-year cumulative dollar totals are reviewed.

Establishing Links Between Alumni Involvement and Annual Giving. Like many educational institutions, MIT had long separated support for alumni relations activities and annual giving into different administrative units. Different staffs worked with different sets of volunteers to achieve goals that were quite different, or so we believed. It is an axiom of alumni relations that effective alumni involvement programs are necessary for successful fundraising from alumni. Many an alumni director has sought to demonstrate this connection. At MIT, as in most schools, the fundraisers typically ignored alumni relations and focused their attention on vigorously and creatively finding new and better ways to ask for gifts, believing that the key to effective fundraising rests in the well-known maxim, "If you don't ask, you don't get."

In the summer of 1988, at the direction of the association board and the recommendation of the senior staff, the MIT alumni relations and annual fund

Table 2.4. MIT Alumni/ae Fund Weekly Progress Report: Week 34—February 13, 1998

	FY 98		FY 97		FY 96	
	Contributions	Contributors	Contributions	Contributors	Contributions	Contributors
Donor Classification						
Repeat alumni/ae (LYBUNTS)	$12,318,530	16,685	$12,595,450	16,098	$11,483,572	15,876
Nonrepeat alumni/ae (SYBUNTS)	$2,551,811	3,314	$2,364,013	2,995	$2,228,567	3,380
First-time alumni/ae	$331,130	972	$83,587	752	$121,259	976
Alumni/ae-related friends						
Widows	$535,744	229	$569,020	206	$1,895,207	245
Others	$1,012,081	92	$751,616	85		
Other friends						
Honoraries	$30,206	15	$53,334	14	$1,022,352	111
Unaffiliated	$600,319	84	$583,441	94		
Nonalumni/ae parents	$115,893	481	$291,466	433	$282,458	350
Totals (exclusive of matching gifts)	$17,495,714	21,872	$17,291,927	20,677	$17,033,415	20,938
Matching Gifts	$525,711	1,310	$586,519	1,528	$476,304	1,495
Overall Total	**$18,021,425**		**$17,878,446**		**$17,509,719**	
Week 34 Totals	$347,503	430	$349,307	428	$179,738	327
Gift Levels						
Less than $25	$5,986	415	$5,330	378	$6,564	471
$25 to $99	$388,241	8,685	$372,422	8,365	$398,968	9,093
$100 to $249	$886,203	7,223	$825,448	6,792	$793,588	6,628
$250 to $499	$512,799	1,826	$482,512	1,731	$462,537	1,656
$500 to $999	$713,080	1,323	$662,587	1,220	$594,055	1,102
$1,000 to $1,999	$794,132	716	$702,046	634	$1,487,334	919
$2,000 to $4,999	$926,432	362	$860,371	339		
$5,000 to $24,999	$2,687,322	301	$2,461,834	265	$2,397,749	256
$25,000 to $49,999	$1,433,852	41	$1,232,481	37	$876,254	27
$50,000 to $99,999	$1,953,420	30	$2,238,014	32	$2,016,346	32
$100,000 and up	$4,900,000	49	$5,200,000	52	$4,800,000	48
Totals (alumni/ae donors only, no matching gifts)	**$15,201,467**	**20,971**	**$15,043,045**	**19,845**	**$13,833,395**	**20,232**

staffs were merged into one integrated alumni activities group under a director of alumni activities who also held the title of director of the alumni fund. It became imperative to understand better the relationship between alumni involvement programs and alumni support of the annual fund.

MIT's annual fund participation in the past ten years has been strong, with our undergraduate alumni participation ranked in 1997 by *U.S. News & World Report* as eighth among research universities; our graduate-only participation compares to the top twenty-five undergraduate institutions in those rankings. Alumni involvement at MIT is a high priority, with 8 percent of our undergraduate alumni and 2.5 percent of our graduate-only alumni holding volunteer positions each year. We felt confident that there was a positive relationship between this exemplary record of alumni giving and the outstanding commitment of involved alumni. We set out to test this assumption.

For purposes of the study, we defined involvement as attendance at events (reunions and an MIT centennial celebration), club membership, or recorded volunteer position. We first tested these involvements against the probability of being a donor, as that was the commonly accepted wisdom. We were disappointed to discover that involved alumni were no more likely to be donors than the general alumni body.

Then we decided to test the assumption that there would be a correlation between "quality" giving and involvement. We defined quality giving in terms of three thresholds of five-year cumulative giving, levels at which we had set annual fund goals—$500, $1,250, and $5,000. When we tested involvement against these quality giving levels, a strong relationship between alumni activities and annual giving behavior became remarkably clear. To verify these results, we tested various subgroups of alumni—types of first MIT degree (graduate or undergraduate), geographic region, and age.

As illustrated in Figure 2.3, we found high correlations between involvement and these giving levels in every case. In fact, simple attendance at events or club membership surprisingly showed a higher correlation than volunteer involvement, suggesting that some volunteers may give time and not money, as anecdotal evidence sometimes supports. Although this research does not show any causal relationships between involvement and giving, the high correlations confirm that the behaviors go hand in hand, and both should be encouraged and supported.

Campaign Case Study: Alumni Fund Visit Program. In the hierarchy of annual fund solicitation techniques, face-to-face contact is the best means to seek upgraded gifts from donors who contribute at higher than nominal dollar amounts. Evidence of this was shown in results of an MIT geographical personal solicitation (PS) program conducted between fiscal years 1980–1984. Each year, there had been five PS programs conducted in different U.S. cities, with the prospects and solicitors drawn from the pool of donors with prior-year gifts of $100 or greater. The upgrade rate in all years exceeded 60 percent, much greater than telephone solicitation, which tends to have a 25 percent upgrade rate. In fiscal year 1985, the pool was increased to donors of at least

Figure 2.3. All Undergraduate Alumni

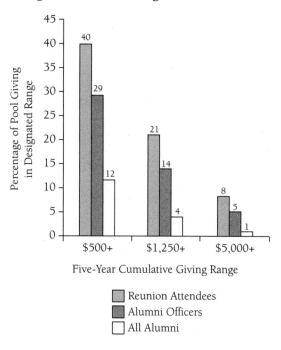

Reunion Attendees
Alumni Officers
All Alumni

$250; 52 percent of the solicited individuals who made a gift in the program expanded their level of support. After a careful audit of PS donors in the fiscal years 1980–1984 to check their gift levels in subsequent years, it was demonstrated that once an upgraded gift was made, the contributor stayed at the increased level.

With evidence that the face-to-face solicitation technique works, a major component of the alumni fund's campaign plan for fiscal years 1987–1992 called for an extensive geographically based face-to-face effort called the Alumni Fund Visit Program (AFVP). In addition, other factors present at MIT argued for implementation of the AFVP plan. For UG alumni, personal solicitations were made only at the twenty-fifth, fortieth, and fiftieth reunion years. Over 40 percent of MIT's alumni were GSEs who were not reached through the reunion program. Finally, the program planned to engage many volunteers—supporters of MIT at more than a nominal level—who would ask large numbers of similar donors for a commitment to MIT substantially greater than ever before contemplated. Further, an analysis of the demographics of MIT alumni with appropriate giving levels demonstrated a geographic distribution that would make this kind of program feasible.

The AFVP, proposed in 1987 to be conducted over the five years of MIT's capital campaign (fiscal years 1988–1992), had the following components:

- Create 35 geographically based solicitation committees for 52 "campaigns."
- Recruit 850 volunteer solicitors.
- Contact 2,700 potential alumni donors.

The estimated results were

- 1,000 upgraded gifts
- Average gift increase of $300
- "Net" gift revenue of $750,000
- Upgrade rate of 67 percent

The actual AFVP results differed somewhat from the proposal. A total of seventy-one AFVP campaigns were conducted, including four in Europe (Zurich and Geneva, Switzerland, London, and Greece) rather than the planned fifty-two. There were 550 volunteer solicitors versus the target of 850. Nearly 2,100 alumni were solicited compared with the objective of 2,700. However, more than $4.3 million was received in gifts, versus the $750,000 goal, and the upgrade rate was 83 percent, much higher than the 67 percent objective.

Future Alumni Fund Research

The consistent growth and vitality of the MIT annual fund is a function of a great many things other than good research data—for example, strong volunteer leadership and involvement (roughly two thousand alumni fund volunteers contribute time and energy to this success); an experienced, professional, and dedicated staff; and loyal and proud alumni. Nevertheless, a critical key to its success over the past fifteen to twenty years has been the consistency of good data applied to setting goals, solving problems, creating new programs, and evaluating ongoing ones. To continue to provide the kind of research support this annual fund has come to rely on, the association is revamping its alumni database (little has changed since 1979) with the expected conversion to a client-server platform by July–August 1998. We expect the flexibility of this new system to allow even better analysis and produce continued outstanding results.

JOSEPH S. COLLINS is director of the Operations and Alumni Fund at the Association of Alumni and Alumnae at the Massachusetts Institute of Technology.

WILLIAM J. HECHT is executive vice president and chief executive officer at the Association of Alumni and Alumnae at the Massachusetts Institute of Technology.

DIANA TILLEY STRANGE is director of special projects and special assistant to the executive vice president at the Association of Alumni and Alumnae at the Massachusetts Institute of Technology.

Results from a project of linked alumni and employer surveys at North Carolina State University were analyzed to explore the comparability of their ratings. A survey of administrators was subsequently undertaken to explore the impact of survey-based assessment information on planning, assessment, curriculum revision, and customer satisfaction at the department and college levels.

Using Surveys of Alumni and Their Employers to Improve an Institution

J. Joseph Hoey, Denise C. Gardner

As the external pressure mounts on institutions to lead a more self-examined life (Ewell, 1984) and to develop more comprehensive approaches to assessing their outcomes, the need to search for valid and reliable indicators of institutional performance has never been greater. In addition to classical measurement considerations, the *believability* and *utility* of the data obtained through assessment processes have been central problems for faculty, administrators, and institutional researchers engaged in this search. What is easy to measure may not be what is most meaningful in measuring program performance. This creates a need for "assessment approaches that produce evidence that relevant parties will find credible, suggestive, and applicable to decisions to be made" (American Association for Higher Education, 1992, p. 3). Alumni and employer surveys have the advantage of ranking high in believability *and* utility for both formative, faculty-driven assessment purposes as well as for summative evaluations at the system or state level (Banta, Lund, Black, and Oblander, 1996). Furthermore, a triangulated approach to assessment that features multiple sources of evaluative data has the advantage of generally yielding a more comprehensive view of the programs being assessed. In recognition of the need for believable and useful assessment data, a linked program of alumni and employer survey research has been moving ahead at North Carolina State University (NC State) since 1993.

Three considerations were decisive in the approach adopted at NC State to surveying alumni and employers. First, due to the primarily technical nature of the institution, we needed an approach that measured commonalities between undergraduate academic preparation and the world of work. Second, in order to understand how to interpret the ratings received, we required a method of assessing the extent of agreement between various raters. Third, to satisfy accreditation requirements, we sought an ongoing program of assessment, one that permitted feedback gained through surveys to be demonstrably incorporated into department or unit plans that have an impact on the operations and outcomes of the institution. Mindful of these considerations, a large-scale approach to seeking feedback from alumni and employers was designed. This chapter will provide an overview of that approach, and will (1) describe the process used to develop survey instruments, (2) detail briefly the logistical aspects and quality assurance steps taken, (3) discuss the similarities and differences in how alumni and employers rated alumni preparation, (4) present findings concerning how alumni and employer survey research data have had a positive impact at NC State, and (5) culminate with a series of lessons learned, which may be instructive for institutions that wish to pursue a similar program of survey research.

Previous Research

The theoretical basis for developing the alumni and employer surveys at NC State was the belief that undergraduate program impact could best be measured by assessing the knowledge, skills, and abilities that connect the academy to the world of work. Mentkowski and Rogers (1993) define several central principles in this connection, based on their experience at Alverno College. These include the need to assess problem-solving and other multidimensional abilities. Similarly, Eveslage (1993) outlines areas of common ground between the academy and the world of work in a summary of relevant theoretical approaches.

Two sets of measurement constructs frequently appear in connected surveys of alumni and employers. One is concerned with evaluating the *relative importance* of a knowledge or skill area to a graduate's professional position as a method for assessing the relevance of curricula (for example, Van Dyke and Williams, 1996). The other centers on assessing the *knowledge and skill levels* of graduates (Banta, 1993). Banta's research is important because it demonstrates that meaningful connections between the academy and the world of work do exist and because it validates the frameworks concerning those connections put forward by Mentkowski and Rogers (1993) and Eveslage (1993).

The second theoretical underpinning for the design of alumni and employer surveys at NC State consists of the groundbreaking work done by Pike (1995, 1996) on validating the relationship between self-reports of student gains and the results of standardized tests of achievement. Pike established that self-reports can to some extent be used as effective indicators of student preparation, especially for mathematical knowledge. Others have agreed with this perspective: Ewell, Lovell, Dressler, and Jones (1993) argue that self-reports may be valid, provided that they show consistent relationships across measures.

Studies that offer comparisons between alumni and employer ratings of alumni preparation (Smith and Wilson, 1992; Womble, 1993) are less frequently found in the literature. Still less attention has been given to attempts at systematic cross-validation of one set of ratings with another (Annis and Rice, 1992; Raymond, 1993). Given the current interest in evaluating academic programs via alumni and employer ratings, such a systematic cross-referencing of ratings on a university-wide basis became an important focus for the survey research program at NC State.

Alumni and Employer Survey Project

This section describes the research from its inception to its completion and then follows with evaluation of the data and a discussion of the implementation of results.

Design and Implementation. The alumni and employer survey project was conceptualized in the fall of 1993 and followed a lengthy process to the reporting stage. Major components of this process are outlined in Table 3.1.

Instruments to assess educational gains from the perspective of the employer (in this case, the direct supervisor) and the perspective of the alumnus or alumna were developed through a highly participatory process at NC State (Hoey, 1995). Researchers in University Planning and Analysis (UPA) organized a morning of faculty focus groups in November 1993. The idea of staging faculty focus groups had been enthusiastically endorsed by the Council of Associate Deans and was subsequently funded by the provost. Fifty-nine faculty members and academic administrators attended, representing every college and school at NC State. A primary goal of the focus groups was to identify overall issues, topics of interest, and methodological concerns that faculty members had about a program of alumni, employer, and graduating senior survey research. Judging from the level of participation, the extensive data obtained, and the subsequent broadening of the university dialogue on assessment issues, the event was considered an overwhelming success.

Data from the faculty focus groups were compiled and shared with all focus group participants. Findings were next reported to the University Institutional Effectiveness Committee. The chair of this committee appointed a

Table 3.1. Process of Creation and Implementation of Alumni and Employer Surveys at North Carolina State

Date	Process
Fall 1993	Instrument creation: faculty focus groups
Spring 1994	Instrument creation: institutional effectiveness committee
Fall 1994	Pilot testing: graduating senior survey
Spring 1995	Pilot testing: alumni survey
Fall 1995	Alumni sample readied
Late fall 1995–spring 1996	Data collection: alumni survey
Late spring–summer 1996	Data collection: employer survey

working group of faculty members to assist UPA with the construction of a series of survey instruments. Using focus group findings as well as the results of an extensive literature search, this working group completed its task in spring 1994. Pilot testing of the graduating senior survey was conducted in fall 1994, followed by pilot testing of the alumni survey in spring 1995.

Both alumni and employer instruments featured an identical core of items on knowledge, skills, and abilities gained through undergraduate programs at this institution. These professional preparation items concerned areas of technical (including computer) skills, communication skills, workplace skills, and professional traits and attitudes. Alumni as well as their direct supervisors were asked to estimate the *importance* of each skill, ability, or area of knowledge to the employee's current work. Alumni were then asked to report on the level of educational *preparation* they had experienced through their programs. Supervisors were asked to rate the knowledge, skills, and abilities of NC State alumni compared with other employees at the same level and in the same capacity. Alumni were also asked to rate the current importance to them of NC State's goals for undergraduate education and to rate how satisfied they were that their undergraduate education had met each goal. The instrument also included items concerned with current employment status, further education status, and suggestions for improvement. To bolster the institution's ability to conduct longitudinal research studies of student growth, development, and outcomes, numerous items from the alumni survey have also been included on other institutional surveys of entering students, sophomores, and graduating seniors.

Methodology, Quality Assurance, and Dissemination. Because the ability to disaggregate survey results to the department level was an important design feature from the start, the alumni survey was administered to baccalaureate degree recipients who graduated from the institution between December 1990 and August 1993, in order to produce sufficient sample size ($N = 7,491$). The instrument was mailed between late fall 1995 and spring 1996 and was followed by the employer survey between late spring and summer 1996.

The entire survey process was designed to include elements that are standard in the survey research literature and that have been shown to contribute to response rate. For the alumni survey, these included two rounds of updating and verifying current alumni addresses; a pilot survey; a custom-designed prenotification card; a first mailing that used a personally addressed cover letter from the chancellor printed on bond, which was mailed first class with a postage-paid business reply envelope included; a custom-designed follow-up card mailed to all who did not respond within two weeks of the first mailing; two subsequent mailings to nonrespondents; and a telephone follow-up to those who had still not responded after three full mailings of the instrument.

This lengthy process resulted in 3,179 usable responses from alumni. Adjusting for known and estimated ineligibles (Lavrakas, 1993), our response rate of 51.1 percent is slightly above the 21 to 50 percent range reported by Banta (1993) as being typical for surveys of this type. On the alumni survey instrument, the researchers requested permission to survey direct supervisors at places of employment. For the 975 alumni who provided contact information, surveys were sent directly to their supervisors, each with one follow-up mailing. Two mailings to employers produced 616 usable responses, a 67.8 percent adjusted response rate.

Data quality is a critical issue in the interpretation of data from the NC State alumni and employer surveys. Measures of the overall margin of error for both surveys were quite good (under 2 percent margin of error). For each survey, items displayed high internal consistency (reliability), with Cronbach alphas of .90 or better. A post hoc comparison of demographic information on the population, mailed sample, and obtained sample (both alumni and employer) revealed no practical significant differences by gender, ethnicity, or year of graduation. Significant differences at the $p = .001$ level were found by college for the alumni survey, but only for one college.

Results were disseminated to the campus community in a number of ways. A series of reports on university-wide results were sent to administrators, deans, associate deans, department heads, and unit heads. These reports were also published on UPA's survey research Web page, located at http://www2.acs.ncsu.edu/UPA/survey/survey.htm. College and departmental analyses, including analyses of any questions inserted by the unit, were sent to the appropriate academic personnel in all cases in which at least ten alumni provided usable responses. Presentations of findings have been made to vice chancellors, deans, the Council on Undergraduate Education, groups of administrative unit heads reporting to vice chancellors for student services and university advancement, and other select groups.

Comparison of Alumni and Employer Ratings. Analyses of data from the alumni and employer surveys proceeded in many stages. To assess the basic rating agreement on an item-by-item basis, an ordinal measure of agreement (Kappa) was used. Low but significant agreement (Kappa = .20 to .36) was found on only seven importance items and one preparation item. To the extent that agreement is evident—mostly in technical, scientific, and mathematical skills—it reinforces Pike's (1995) finding that mathematical skills may be more reliably assessed using self-reports than other skill areas.

Although the ratings of alumni and their direct supervisors showed few signs of agreement at the individual level, a considerable extent of agreement on ratings was evident at an aggregated (university) level. In a comparison of mean ratings, both alumni and employers accorded high levels of importance to professional preparation in general. A surprise in the results of this survey was that responding alumni rated the level of their professional preparation considerably *lower* than did employers. Moreover, this was a consistent finding across virtually all items concerned with professional preparation on the survey instruments.

Gap score analysis. In an approach promulgated by Noel-Levitz and referred to as *performance gap scores* (USAGroup Noel-Levitz, 1996), the differences (gap scores) were assessed between how important alumni and employers felt a skill or ability was to the job and the extent to which NC State graduates possessed that skill or ability. In an extension of this technique, overall gap scores were then developed based on the differences between alumni and employer gap scores. *T*-tests were run to ascertain the deviation from zero of the overall gap scores. For six items, a lack of significant difference from zero in the overall gap scores was found. Those items are *overall technical knowledge, ability to apply math skills, foreign language skills, skills gained through research or internship experience, ability to define problems,* and *ability to work under pressure.* Foreign language skills were generally rated of lower importance by both alumni and employers, and Pike's (1995, 1996) findings would lead us to expect more accurate self-assessment in math skills. For the other items, it may be that the real-world experience acquired by alumni since graduation led them to rate importance and preparation in a similar fashion to their work supervisors.

Factor analysis. To explore the possibility of underlying consensus in the patterns of ratings given by alumni and employers, indices of survey items were formed by multiplying importance ratings by preparation ratings. This was done separately on the ratings from employers and from alumni. These indices were then subjected to factor analysis, using procedures recommended by Hatcher (1994). Varimax rotation of alumni and employer data sets yielded a three-factor solution for indices of employer items and a four-factor solution for indices of alumni items. For employer ratings, we labeled these factors *work skills and abilities; communication, interpersonal, and conceptual skills;* and *technical and scientific skills.* For alumni ratings, we labeled the four resulting factors *work skills and abilities, planning and problem-solving skills, communication and interpersonal skills,* and *technical and scientific skills.* It is worth noting the agreement on separate factors for work skills and abilities, and for technical and scientific skills. The only substantive difference found was that responding alumni differentiated between communication and interpersonal skills on the one hand and planning and problem-solving skills on the other, and responding employers made no such differentiation. Thus, a basic consensus on ratings between alumni and employers became apparent. The isolation of three to four basic factors further supports Banta's (1993) findings and again validates the theoretical framework put forward for this research concerning the need to assess those skills that connect NC State to the world of work (Mentkowski and Rogers, 1993; Eveslage, 1993).

Regression analysis. One of the goals of our survey research project was to evaluate survey ratings given by both alumni and employers. Originally, our purpose was to determine how valid alumni ratings were by using employer ratings of professional preparation as a reference, as employer ratings have the advantage of being more believable to many constituencies both on and off campus. To arrive at such a determination, we regressed the weighted factors (derived through factor analysis of the indices of survey items, as explained above) against the self-reported salary levels of alumni. The weights were calculated from the factor loadings and were assumed to be random effects. Salary was used in this context as the most accurate available indicator of alumni skill level and competency. The logic of this approach is that more accurate ratings of importance and preparation should act as better predictors of salary level. To control for salary differences by discipline, college was added to the model. Gender and ethnicity were also entered into the model to control for vagaries of the marketplace in salary levels. University grade point average (GPA) was entered into the model to control for its possible effect as a predictor, as was year of graduation. The analysis was done using general linear models and type III sums of squares for testing purposes (testing the marginal contribution of the variables to the model). Results are given in Table 3.2.

Analysis revealed that the regression model that included alumni ratings (R^2 = .348) proved quite similar to the model that included employer ratings (R^2 = .350) in capacity to predict alumni salaries. College (as a proxy for discipline), gender, GPA range, and year of graduation (as a proxy for length of time on the job) provided the lion's share of explanatory power in both models. Ethnicity was not significant in either model and was deleted from further consideration. Survey-based factors significant (at $p \leq .05$) in the salary prediction equation for alumni included *communication and interpersonal skills* and *technical and scientific skills*. For employers, survey-based factors significant in the salary prediction equation included *communication, interpersonal, and conceptual skills* and *technical and scientific skills*. Commonalties are evident: both responding alumni and employers opine that communication and interpersonal skills as well as technical and scientific skills are significant determinants of alumni salaries. At the very least, the results demonstrate areas of agreement on those skill sets that connect academe and the world of work. The differences observed may be of degree rather than of basic substance. For a technically oriented institution such as NC State, these findings provide validation of what employers of engineers and other scientific or technical disciplines

Table 3.2. Results of Regression Analysis on Factor-Based Indices of Alumni and Employer Ratings on Importance and Preparation

Variable in Equation	F Value (Type III SS)	Pr > F (Type III SS)	Model R-square
Alumni			.348
College	99.93	.0001	
Gender	13.57	.0001	
GPA range	9.45	.0082	
Year of graduation	25.86	.0001	
Communication and interpersonal skills	4.04	.0245	
Technical and scientific skills	4.09	.0237	
Employers			.350
College	147.53	.0001	
Gender	16.49	.0001	
GPA range	10.74	.0038	
Year of graduation	22.63	.0001	
Communication and conceptual skills	5.95	.0063	
Technical and scientific skills	4.41	.0187	

have been saying: technical skills are important, but communication and inter-personal skills are also vital attributes for all knowledge workers (for example, see Saperstein, 1997, at http://www.asee.org/assessment/html/saperstein.htm).

Summary of Findings. In general, employers of NC State's alumni who were surveyed in this study report that graduates are fairly well prepared for the important aspects of their jobs. Moreover, alumni have highly developed computer and mathematical-scientific technical skills (as would be expected from a university such as NC State) and may even be better prepared in those areas than necessary. Nonetheless, employers feel our graduates are somewhat less than optimally prepared to deal with aspects of professional practice such as defining and solving problems, making decisions under pressure, and adjusting to new job demands. Generally, alumni rated themselves as slightly less prepared overall than did their employers. Both groups rated leadership and management skills as important but gave relatively low ratings to NC State alumni in this area relative to other dimensions assessed.

A basic reason for conducting comparative research on alumni and employer ratings was to ascertain whether alumni ratings may be used as valid proxies for employer ratings of alumni performance. It is important to point out what our study revealed: Evidently, supervisors evaluate skills and abilities from a different standpoint than alumni, and the evidence suggests that even though the underlying conceptualization of skills and abilities is similar between the two groups, the ratings are essentially noncomparable. This means that if this finding holds up in subsequent research, institutions will need to continue to do both kinds of assessments to get a comprehensive picture of student outcomes.

Although alumni and employer ratings are not directly comparable, both have been used at the college and department or unit level to get a clearer picture of student outcomes, and in many cases to effect positive change for the institution. The sizable sample obtained for the alumni survey ($N = 3,179$) allowed disaggregation to the department level in all but a few departments with less than ten respondents, whereas the sample obtained from employers ($N = 616$) was disaggregated to the college level only.

Impact of Project

The curricular impact of providing survey-based assessment results to colleges and departments at NC State is discussed in this section.

Methodology and Implementation. For administrators, the bottom line in assessment research is certainly its measurable and positive effect on edu-cational and administrative processes. To ascertain the impact on colleges and departments of providing student, alumni, and employer survey information, we conducted an electronic survey of department and unit administrators in January 1998. We sent the instrument to a population of eighty associate deans, associate vice chancellors, department heads, and directors at NC State. We received forty-four usable responses (seven associate deans, one associate vice chancellor, twenty-seven department heads, and nine administrative unit directors), for a response rate of 55 percent. Although this rate precludes generalization of findings to the population of interest, the data nevertheless offer substantial insights into the impact of a survey-based assessment program at a major Research I institution and demonstrate the wide extent to which the survey research program is having a positive effect on the university's ability to become a more self-regarding institution (Ewell, 1984).

The instrument consisted of questions that followed a national set of guidelines for the improvement of organizational effectiveness, the Malcolm Baldrige National Quality Award *1997 Criteria for Performance Excellence* (as cited in North Carolina Quality Leadership Foundation, 1997). Respondents were asked to rate each component of NC State's survey research program (entering student, graduating senior, alumni-employer) on each area. The questions were primarily concerned with the degree to which the provision of survey information had enabled units to assess their performance; what the units had done to realign, change, or improve their unit's performance on the basis of survey information; and the extent to which the provision of survey information had enabled units to use externally generated information to maintain and improve the currency and flexibility of their programs.

Several open-ended items were also included, to allow respondents to describe more fully how the information provided had affected their units (including providing examples of specific actions in which survey information was used), which of the reports were most useful, and how the reporting process could be improved. In addition, the respondents were asked to provide any additional comments they cared to make concerning survey information. Although palpable impact on the institution is evident from other components of NC State's survey research program, results reported here reflect only the findings related to the impact of alumni and employer surveys.

Assessing Unit Performance. In a series of seven items, survey respondents were asked to rate the extent to which alumni and employer survey information had enabled them to assess effectively the performance of their department or unit. Table 3.3 shows the percentage who indicated that alumni and employer surveys had been *moderately* or *very useful* to their college, department, or unit for each purpose.

Determining key program, activity, and service features and developing or revising strategic plans were the two areas in which alumni and employer surveys were found to be most useful. One respondent noted, "My general response is that all the surveys are giving us empirical foundations on which to develop our plans and goals." Two other respondents noted the need for survey trend data to assist their assessment efforts. One commented, "Trend information would greatly help, also peer comparisons." The other said, "A longer series of surveys is required to confidently track and change."

Three other respondents proffered insights concerning the level at which the greatest impact of survey data would be felt. One commented, "Departmental reports are most useful." Another offered, "Department had full discussion of alumni results." The third remarked, "In order for the reports to directly affect our behavior and plans, it has to be taken down to the departmental level."

Table 3.3. Usefulness of Alumni and Employer Surveys
for Planning and Assessment

Survey Item	Percentage Reporting That Alumni-Employer Surveys Were Moderately or Very Useful for This Purpose
Determine key program, activity, and service features and their relative importance and value to employers, alumni, students, the general public, and other stakeholders	49
Develop or revise strategic plans, including such factors as your target markets and stakeholders, the learning environment, opportunities and threats, the capabilities of your department or unit, and supplier or partner capabilities	49
Have more open discussions and sharing of information among members of your department or unit	39
Integrate the information you gained from survey findings and reports into measurements that can be used to track and improve the performance of your department or unit	36
Track your department or unit performance relative to your strategic plan	32
Compare your department's or unit's performance with that of similar departments or units at this or other institutions	30
Assess your current performance relative to your past performance	26

Changing, Realigning, and Improving Department or Unit Performance. The next series of items requested information on whether alumni and employer survey reports had been used as a basis for changing, realigning, or improving departmental or unit performance. Results are shown in Table 3.4. The most frequently reported actions that were taken on the basis of survey-based assessment results were to update strategic and action plans for the next cycle and to follow up with stakeholders on programs, activities, and services.

In an open-ended follow-up to these items, respondents were asked to describe examples of specific activities, projects, or other actions in which they had used survey information to realign, change, or improve their department or unit. The numerous responses received fell into three thematic categories: curriculum revision; student advising; and improving planning processes, including planning for reaccreditation.

Curriculum revision. Eleven comments alluded to various curricular initiatives and changes that had been put into place as a result of survey information gained. Comments included

"A capstone course was developed during the first year of senior and alumni surveys—findings from those surveys have helped us make changes in the capstone course in response to identified needs."

**Table 3.4. Actions Taken on the Findings
of Alumni and Employer Surveys**

Survey Item	Percentage Reporting That Action Was Taken in This Area on the Basis of Alumni-Employer Surveys Results
Update and improve strategic and action plans for the next planning cycle	33
Follow up with students, alumni, and employers on programs, activities, and services as a result of what you learned from the surveys	31
Set direction for your department or unit and seek future opportunities; set higher targets for your department's or unit's performance	24
Reorganize the work of your department or unit to enable you to meet current and changing stakeholder and operational requirements	24
Improve your performance-measurement capabilities in the future	21

"Enhanced writing/communication components of coursework, recognized need to increase business and economics skill levels among undergraduates."

"We are also reconsidering the undergraduate and graduate curricula in light of what employers indicate they want of graduates."

"Incorporation of more problem solving into courses. Addition of courses in professionalism and ethics. Addition of course exercises that require teamwork."

"More emphasis on evaluating writing in our undergraduate curricula. We have become aware [of]/ concerned with the need to expose our students to the world of fine arts."

"Development of new concentrations identified by students as important areas for development of competencies in technical agriculture. Faculty appointments have been adjusted to provide more opportunities for extension faculty to teach and interact with students in the extension option."

Advising. Several comments detailed how departments had made revisions to their advising processes as a result of alumni and employer feedback. Comments included

"An associate department head for academic affairs has been appointed to oversee and coordinate all academic and advising matters at the undergraduate and graduate levels."

"Our emphasis on advising minority students has been strengthened."

"Alumni surveys have been useful in identifying problems related to advising, communication, and curriculum."

"Appointed new undergraduate coordinator and agreed on goal of improving advising and building a stronger feeling of ownership among faculty for the undergraduate program."

Planning. A number of comments related to how departmental or unit-planning processes had been affected positively by the information supplied in alumni and employer survey reports. These included

"Departmental strategic plan included improving student support services in light of alumni survey findings."
"Employer surveys have contributed to our planning for, [for example,] implementation of the writing and speaking general education requirements."
"Preparing faculty for the realities of ABET 2000 [engineering accreditation criteria], which is outcomes based."
"In the process of working . . . to align information collected in these surveys with information needed to meet ABET Criteria 2000."
"Our strategic planning process will now center on how to focus the Alumni Association on those things that alums have said they want (such as continued career-planning assistance and professional development opportunities). We also funded a .5 FTE position to work directly with alumni in providing those resources they said they want. For example, we offered a pilot regional career fair for young alumni in Charlotte, where we pulled together 167 alums and 23 corporations. We had great feedback, so we will do one in the Triad next year."

Scanning the Environment. The next section of the survey contained four items concerned with the extent to which alumni and employer survey information increased the ability of departments and units to use externally generated information to maintain and improve the currency and flexibility of their programs. Responses are given in Table 3.5. The most notable finding among these items is the extent to which departments and units found alumni and employer survey information useful for obtaining direct feedback from their customers and stakeholders. This was an avowed purpose of the alumni and employer surveys from the outset, and it appears to have been met.

Few follow-up comments were provided on this section, although one respondent did note that college-level questions contained in an insert to the alumni survey provided by far the most important information and were used by the college in a comprehensive review. Another respondent noted that their department was developing a core course focused on leadership and group dynamics as a result of employers' expressed needs for graduates to have skills in leading public groups in decision making.

How Have Reports Been Most Useful? The chief reason cited for the usefulness of reports derived from alumni and employer surveys had to do with the believable, experienced, and in-depth perspective that alumni and their direct supervisors are able to offer. Representative comments in this vein included

**Table 3.5. Usefulness of Information for Maintaining
and Improving Flexibility**

Survey Item	Percentage Reporting That Alumni-Employer Surveys Were Moderately or Very Useful for This Purpose
Take into account the needs and expectations of key stakeholders as you provide leadership for your department or unit	46
Update, keep current, or improve your ability to listen to and learn from your stakeholders and markets	42
Address current and potential impacts of your programs, activities, services, facilities, and operations on community, state, and society	32
Anticipate public concerns	29

"Alumni/employer: gives additional feedback from the individuals/groups in the best position to judge the effectiveness/quality of our programs."

"Senior and alumni surveys tell us about success/problems from a population that probably is honest in reporting and that has perceived there to be little to lose by being honest."

"Alumni: they are our best evaluators after they've had time to reflect on the value of their education to their lives."

"The alumni report has enabled us (Career Planning and Placement) to make presentations to corporations, so that they may modify their hiring criteria in this tight market. With this analysis, we are providing a level of service to some high-quality corporate customers of ours that they cannot get anywhere else."

"In regional hiring workshops for employers, we used the findings on young alumni and employer opinions about skill sets, and employee training and development programs that are needed. This gave us a way of generating outreach to employers. A whole section of our workbook uses the findings to discuss how to hire, evaluate skills, and retain graduates by providing appropriate professional development."

Many comments noted that reports were most useful when the results were disaggregated to the departmental level. Typical comments included

"College/department level reports. Focused reports done for alumni/employer survey."

"The ones that give departmental info and compare to both college and university."

"Departmental surveys . . . This information has provided the department and committees involved with undergraduate and graduate education a valuable tool to monitor the opinions of graduates."

"More surveying done at the program, not the university, level would be more useful."

Other departments use the information from alumni and employer survey reports to confirm their perceptions of the market: "Because it verified what we thought was true."

The importance of having trend information from multiple administrations of the surveys over time was underscored by an associate dean who commented: "Although the alumni survey has been least useful, it can become the most useful if repeated for more recent alumni. We are interested in post-1995 graduates."

How Could Alumni and Employer Survey Data Be Provided in a More Useful Fashion? A final open-ended question asked respondents to provide feedback on how survey information could be made more useful for their department or unit. Responses fell into several broad areas:

Six respondents directed UPA to continue to provide disaggregated data at the department or unit level and to continue including respondents' written comments. One of the respondents summed it up this way: "The departmental reports and summary of comments relevant to department are most useful."

Five respondents indicated that more customization of survey items to department- or unit-specific questions would provide the greatest benefit. For example, one respondent advised UPA to "tailor the questions to the needs and concerns in the department and permit the department to ask more questions and direct questions about specific topics of interest in the department." Three other respondents affirmed the need to continue working closely with departments and units and listening to their data needs. For example, one associate dean advised: "Continue interacting with us to ensure questions meet college and departmental needs."

Three respondents requested comparative data from other departments at comparable institutions. As one associate dean phrased it, "Obtain similar info from our peer institutions for comparisons. What are the benchmarks?"

Another theme that emerged concerned reduction of information. Respondents advised UPA to simplify the presentation of information, to continue to provide executive summaries, but to put disaggregated data in tables on the Web. As one respondent put it, "I like getting the executive summaries. Putting the rest of the material on the Web would work best for me. The full reports are long."

UPA had already begun implementing some of these suggestions, such as disseminating printed copies of shorter summary reports and putting more detailed reports (along with tables of responses) on the Web. The next cycle of alumni-employer surveys is well under way, and input from academic personnel was again solicited to ensure that departmental questions on survey inserts meet their needs for assessment information.

Summary of Findings. From project planning to ultimate effect on the institution, the impact of alumni and employer and other survey research–

based assessment is evident at NC State. Academic departments are sharing survey information and discussing the results among themselves. They are incorporating feedback from alumni and employers into revisions of strategic and action plans for their units. They are also using the data to understand the needs expressed by their customers and stakeholders and subsequently are altering or creating new courses, curriculum emphases, and services that address these needs.

Of all the surveys included in the NC State program of survey research, alumni and employer surveys have been singled out by departments as having the most believable and unbiased points of view and therefore some of the most valuable information for program improvement. Still, only one-fifth to one-third of responding units had taken direct action on the basis of alumni and employer survey findings. Several reasons may be advanced for this. First and foremost is the fact that departments and units also find other annual surveys (first-year orientation survey, graduating senior) done by UPA to be of utility for planning and assessment purposes. Several iterations of these other instruments have taken place, and trend analyses are available. Second, department and unit heads noted that survey information is only one of the information sources they use in making academic-planning and resource allocation decisions. Third, many departments received high marks for their efforts from both alumni and employers and may not have felt compelled to alter their courses at this point. Fourth, things tend to move slowly in academe, and faculty need time to ponder findings before proceeding with changes to a curriculum. Finally, comparison of results across time was also a prevalent request, one that entails collecting alumni and employer survey data on a longitudinal basis for trend analysis. On a positive note, departments requested that the information continue to be provided in a format in which they can compare their results to other departments, to their college, and to the university as a whole in order to maximize the usefulness of these data.

Lessons Learned

From the NC State experience, several lessons can be inferred for future alumni and employer surveys:

- Secure adequate funding and support from administration for your assessment program.
- Know what you want to measure, at what level of aggregation, and why it is important information. This may involve a reexamination of your institution's mission statement, strategic goals, and objectives. It will most certainly mean that the intended student learning outcomes (for example, a general education) will need to be very clearly specified.
- Plan for and actively seek collective faculty input on the content of alumni and employer surveys. Obtaining employer input on potential items is also critical. This means devoting sufficient time and resources toward obtaining

that input. A benefit of early faculty and employer involvement is that they then have a stake in the project and are more likely to use the results.

• Where resources allow, use a large-enough sample size such that findings may be disaggregated to the department or unit level. Information that is useful at this level is clearly the most important data in the long run, as it is these data that help departments and units assess their own performance and the effect of innovations they introduce.

• Where resources allow, use custom designs or department or unit inserts to the main survey that allow departments to collect specific information of value to them.

• Plan and pilot-test survey items thoroughly, because the usefulness of the data will be directly related to the validity and reliability of the instruments used, and the kinds of policy or program questions to be answered will need to be thought through and explicitly addressed at the planning stages for the data to be of maximum usefulness for decision making.

• Address issues of data access up front. Results of university-level survey items should be openly available. Results of specific department- or unit-level survey items (for example, on departmental inserts) should be disseminated to that department or unit only.

• Consider working with peer institutions on cross-institutional studies, to allow for benchmarking comparisons.

• Keep reports simple, and make data and reports widely available (for example, via the Web) in a format that departments and units can easily access.

• Begin now! The highest benefits of a survey program do not really begin to accrue until several cycles of data collection have taken place. It takes at least three rounds of data collection for trend analysis to begin.

References

American Association for Higher Education. *Principles of Good Practice for Assessing Student Learning.* Washington, D.C.: American Association for Higher Education, 1992.

Annis, A. W., and Rice, R. R. "An Assessment of an Economics and Business Department: Surveys of Graduates and Their Supervisors." Paper presented at the annual forum of the Association for Institutional Research, Atlanta, May 1992.

Banta, T. W. "Critique of a Method for Surveying Employers." *Association for Institutional Research Professional File,* no. 47. Tallahassee, Fla.: Association for Institutional Research, 1993.

Banta, T. W., Lund, J. P., Black, K. E., and Oblander, F. W. *Assessment in Practice.* San Francisco: Jossey-Bass, 1996.

Eveslage, S. A. "The Case for Workplace Assessment." Paper presented at the meeting of the American Association for Higher Education, Chicago, June 1993.

Ewell, P. T. *The Self-Regarding Institution: Information for Excellence.* Boulder, Colo.: National Center for Higher Education Management Systems, 1984.

Ewell, P. T., Lovell, C. D., Dressler, P., and Jones, D.P.A. *Preliminary Study of the Feasibility and Utility for National Policy of Instructional Good Practice Indicators in Undergraduate Education.* Boulder, Colo.: National Center for Higher Education Management Systems, 1993.

Hatcher, R. *A Step-by-Step Guide to Using the SAS System for Factor Analysis and Structural Equations Modeling.* Cary, N.C.: SAS Institute, 1994.

Hoey, J. J. "Assuring Faculty Input into Institutional Effectiveness and Assessment Processes at North Carolina State University: An Application of Focus Group Methodology." Paper presented at the annual forum of the Association for Institutional Research, Boston, May 1995.

Lavrakas, P. J. *Telephone Survey Methods: Sampling, Selection, and Supervision.* Thousand Oaks, Calif.: Sage, 1993.

Mentkowski, M., and Rogers, G. "Using Workplace Feedback to Assess Educational Programs." Paper presented at the meeting of the American Association for Higher Education, Chicago, June 1993.

North Carolina Quality Leadership Foundation. *Education Performance Excellence Criteria.* Raleigh: North Carolina Quality Leadership Foundation, 1997.

Pike, G. R. "The Relationship Between Self-Reports of College Experiences and Achievement Test Scores." *Research in Higher Education,* 1995, *36* (1), 1–21.

Pike, G. R. "Limitations of Using Students' Self-Reports of Academic Development as Proxies for Traditional Achievement Measures." *Research in Higher Education,* 1996, *37* (1), 89–114.

Raymond, M. A. (ed.). "Preparing Graduates for the Workforce: The Role of Business Education." *Journal of Education for Business,* 1993, *68* (4), 202–206.

Saperstein, L. "Outcomes Measures and Performance Assessment: An Industrial Perspective." Panel presented at the National Conference on Outcomes Assessment, Washington, D.C., September 1997. Proceedings online at http://www.asee.org/assessments/html /saperstein.htm.

Smith, D., and Wilson, H. "The Development and Assessment of Personal Transferable Skills During Work-Based Placements." *Assessment and Evaluation in Higher Education,* 1992, *17* (3), 195–208.

USAGroup Noel-Levitz. *1996 National Student Satisfaction Report.* Iowa City, Iowa: USA Group Noel-Levitz, 1996.

Van Dyke, J., and Williams, G. W. "Involving Graduates and Employers in Assessment of a Technology Program." In T. W. Banta, J. P. Lund, K. E. Black, and F. W. Oblander (eds.), *Assessment in Practice.* San Francisco: Jossey-Bass, 1996.

Womble, M. N. "Assessment of Competencies for Computer Information Systems Curricula." *Delta Pi Epsilon Journal,* 1993, *35* (2), 69–85.

J. JOSEPH HOEY is director of assessment at the Georgia Institute of Technology.

DENISE C. GARDNER is senior research analyst in institutional research and planning at the Georgia Institute of Technology.

As tuition costs continue to rise, colleges are relying more heavily on alumni to help finance undergraduate education. This chapter evaluates the success of one program, the Cornell Tradition, in encouraging current undergraduate aid recipients to give back to the university after graduation.

What Makes a Difference: Evaluating the Cornell Tradition Program

Yuko Mulugetta, Scott Nash, Susan H. Murphy

Over the past two decades, private institutions have had to rely more than ever on the support of their alumni, particularly for undergraduate financial aid programs. Since the 1970s, tuition has continued to rise faster than both inflation and average family income. Federal and state grant aid to students has not kept pace with this rapid increase in prices. As a result, students have experienced a major increase in their undergraduate debt levels, and colleges have made up the remaining difference by devoting more institutional resources to financial aid (Hauptman, 1990; Gladieux and Hauptman, 1995). Recycling tuition revenue in the form of institutional grant support has reached alarming levels at many institutions (Hubbell, 1995; Lapovsky, 1996), stimulating major efforts to raise endowment funds and gifts for financial aid programs from alumni. These efforts have become critically important for private institutions struggling to maintain a healthy financial state.

Prospective students and their parents responded to changes in the economics of higher education by becoming increasingly sensitive to college costs and financial aid issues. Consequently, even many selective institutions face serious competition in attracting top students (Mulugetta, Saleh, and Mulugetta, 1997). Recent announcements by Princeton, Yale, and Stanford about major restructuring of their financial aid programs suggest that this competition is likely to become more intense in the near future (Stecklow, 1998; "Stanford Increases. . . ," 1998; Gose, 1998).

Contributions of Alumni

Given today's competitive academic marketplace, the role of alumni extends beyond making financial contributions to their alma mater. At many colleges and universities, alumni play an important role in the recruitment and admissions process. They also assist current undergraduates by acting as mentors and sources of internships and other job opportunities. Motivated alumni may act as effective ambassadors for their alma mater by increasing the recognition and prestige of the institution in their home communities.

The importance of alumni contributions to private institutions, therefore, raises some critical questions: What, if anything, can institutions do to nurture or reinforce the values that will encourage undergraduates to support their institution either financially or through their volunteer efforts after graduation? Can the university, through its institutional commitment and programs, provide models of active citizenship and participation in community service? Most studies of alumni donors suggest that undergraduate experiences such as participation in extracurricular activities are much weaker predictors of alumni activities than other characteristics such as gender, age, and current income (Brittingham and Pezzulo, 1990; Young and Fischer, 1996). Although a positive attitude toward one's alma mater is assumed to be a prerequisite of alumni giving, how this attitude is nurtured while alumni are still in college has not been studied in much detail. Our research takes a closer look at these questions.

Our study has two purposes. First, we attempt to conceptualize a model in which the institution plays an active role in fostering the values and abilities of undergraduates that will encourage them to be active, engaged alumni in the future. Second, we test this model by using Cornell University data and examine the effect of participation in the Cornell Tradition, an undergraduate special-recognition program, on young alumni behavior.

Input-Environment-Outcome Model

Our conceptual model depends heavily on Alexander Astin's Input-Environment-Outcome (I-E-O) model, with some modifications. According to Astin, "*Inputs* refer to the characteristics of the student at the time of initial entry to the institution; *environment* refers to the various programs, policies, faculty, peers, and educational experiences to which the student is exposed; and *outcome* refers to the student's characteristics after exposure to the environment." (Astin, 1993, p. 7). The I-E-O model, therefore, evaluates the impact of certain college environments on the postgraduation characteristics or behavior of students by examining whether alumni developed differently after being exposed to a particular college environment compared with the predicted outcome were they not exposed to such conditions. A previous study has demonstrated that the I-E-O model can be a powerful tool for examining how undergraduate activities and experiences affect alumni behavior (Young and Fischer, 1996).

Although the I-E-O model has been applied successfully to research on educational outcomes, we believe that one of the weaknesses of the model stems from a broad, rather vague conceptualization of the institution's role in the I-E-O process. In the I-E-O model, institutions play the role of the creator of the environment. According to Astin, "These institutional characteristics tend to create particular environmental circumstances—Research Orientation, Student Orientation, Humanities Orientation, certain peer group factors—that in turn affect student outcomes" (Astin, 1993, p. 414).

Input-Commitment-Environment-Outcome Model

Defining an institution as the environmental creator enables us to capture the broad role of the institution in producing environments that have an impact on the formation of specific characteristics of a variety of groups, for example, faculty groups, peer groups, and so forth. The overall environment, as mediated by a number of these different groups, in turn affects cognitive and noncognitive characteristics of individual students. This definition, however, tends to obscure the role of the university as an active player not only in creating an environment but also in reinforcing the effect of that environment on student outcomes in the direction the institution intends. What is needed therefore is a means of taking into account the sustained intention, or commitment, of the institution to achieve its defined goals. Some colleges and universities seem more engaged than others in their efforts to shape student outcomes in ways that reflect institutional purposes. We propose a new concept that successfully captures the extent to which the institution plays an active role in reinforcing the intended environmental effects on students during their college years and beyond.

In the modified model, therefore, we introduce such a concept—*institutional commitment*. Institutional commitment is defined as the degree to which the institution sustains its intention and acts to produce defined student outcomes by creating and reinforcing particular environmental circumstances. In our view, the concept of institutional commitment is critically important in explaining why some institutions are more successful in affecting student outcomes in intended ways than other institutions. The concept also enables us to examine why, under the same institutional environment, students who participated in particular programs realize more desirable outcomes than their peers who did not participate. The challenge, which we discuss below, is to separate those aspects of the environment that are largely created and reinforced by the institution from those that are primarily self-produced by the student or students.

An example may help readers understand more clearly what we mean by institutional commitment. Suppose an institutional goal is to instill in undergraduates the value of alumni financial support for the university. There are a number of ways the university can do this. The simplest and least expensive way may be just noting the importance of alumni giving in the campus paper and other university publications. A further step might be to invite an alumni donor to speak to current students about the value of staying connected to one's alma mater. Beyond this, the institution could provide students with scholarships named after donors to exemplify the importance of financial support from alumni. Furthermore, the institution could create opportunities for scholarship recipients to meet donors personally to reinforce the value and importance of an intergenerational connection. At each step, the institution increases its active role and commitment by both creating the environment and reinforcing its effect on students, with the intention that these students will grow into active, committed alumni donors in the future.

Our model, the Input-Commitment-Environment-Outcome (I-C-E-O) model, is presented in Figure 4.1. Inputs refer to the students' demographic characteristics at the time they entered the university. As we have noted, environmental concepts present more of a challenge. In a within-institution study such as this one, the students all share a similar macroenvironment. The problem arises in that any particular student's environment is to some extent self-produced and the result of the individual's choices. In other words, when viewed from one perspective, an activity like joining a fraternity is an environmental concept, but from another perspective it is an outcome. Consequently, as Astin has noted, there is always a certain degree of unavoidable ambiguity in self-produced environmental factors (Astin, 1991, pp. 83–84).

To further complicate matters, postbaccalaureate experiences, such as employment and graduate school, can be considered environmental factors or outcomes. Although it can be argued that employment and graduate school experiences are either outcomes of undergraduate college experiences or self-produced, in alumni research, both need to be treated as major environmental conditions that significantly influence alumni behavior, as indicated by Young and Fischer's 1996 study. Volkwein and others (1989) as well as Connolly and Blanchette (1986) present the twin concepts of *financial capacity* and *motivation* as key predictors of alumni's gift-giving behavior. The institution, through its commitment to students, shapes the environment in ways that directly affect motivation. For example, the beneficiaries of special programs may be moved by a feeling of social or personal obligation to support the program when they become financially able. As Fitch (1987) has pointed out, social obligation is a major motivator for service. In the end, environmental variables need to be identified and examined in the context of these final outcome variables.

In the I-C-E-O model, institutional commitment plays a key role in producing intended student outcomes by creating and reinforcing particular environmental circumstances. Because the institution acts as more than just a passive creator of the environment in this model, we are able to conceptualize its role in such a way that the commitment to students takes place in an integrated, comprehensive manner not only during their college years but also after graduation. Integration is a critical operational element in the commitment strategy. It ensures that the various components of a program are mutually reinforcing over both the long and the short term and that they bear an obvious relationship to program outcomes and goals. For example, rewarding

Figure 4.1. Input-Commitment-Environment-Outcome (I-C-E-O) Model

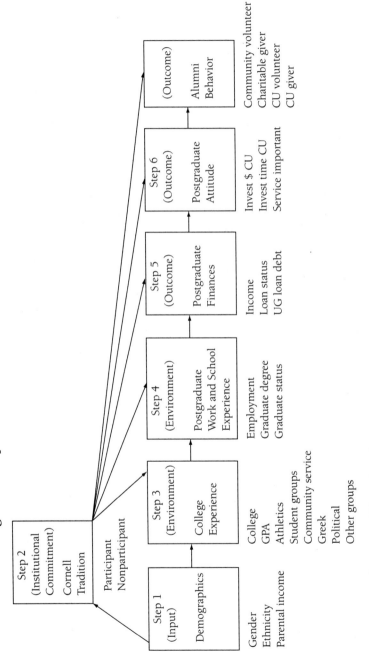

Note: CU = Cornell University, UG = undergraduate

working students by replacing student loans with grant aid encourages initiative, personal responsibility, and the positive value of hard work. Furthermore, this serves to improve the financial capabilities of alumni after graduation as well as their awareness of the importance of financial contributions from donors. By establishing and supporting alumni networks, the institution can provide tangible assistance to help current students and alumni land the job or find the graduate program where their talents are optimally used while at the same time nurturing continued contact between alumni, current students, and the institution. All these program components benefit students while encouraging long-term support of the program and the institution.

Using the I-C-E-O model, we will examine the impact of the Cornell Tradition program by comparing the postgraduate volunteer activities and financial donations of alumni who were Tradition participants with alumni who were nonparticipants.

Cornell Tradition Program

The Cornell Tradition is a special-recognition program that offers six hundred fellowships each year to a select group of Cornell undergraduates, which represents approximately 5 percent of the undergraduate student population. The Cornell Tradition was founded in 1983 and was launched by an anonymous gift of $7 million dollars. This gift was a result of a concern that rapidly rising levels of student debt would discourage many promising students from attending the university, going on to graduate school, or pursuing careers in the nonprofit sector. The Tradition program awards fellowships worth up to $2,500 per year (increasing to $3,500 per year for the 1998–99 academic year) to needy students who have demonstrated a strong commitment to working while in school to help pay for their education, to community service, and to academic achievement. These awards reduce the student loan debt a student would otherwise incur in obtaining a Cornell degree (Murphy and Mulugetta, 1994).

At its creation, six goals were set for the Cornell Tradition program. One of these goals emphasizes the importance of giving back to one's alma mater. The program encourages and motivates fellows to ensure the continuance of the Tradition through future service and financial assistance to the program and university, as well as emphasizing the importance of being an active and engaged citizen. On a conceptual level, the Cornell Tradition represents a major commitment on the part of the university to program participants, with the expectation that fellows will reciprocate in the future. This reciprocity represents the social obligation component of the program. On an operational level, the Tradition is an integrated program in that all of its components, described below, are designed to complement and reinforce one another. This is reflected in the program's mission statement:

> The Cornell Tradition strives to encourage and support lifestyles that integrate a strong work ethic, public service, and academic achievement by rewarding stu-

dents who exemplify these characteristics with recognition and financial support for their education. The program encourages Cornell Tradition Fellows to unify around these common commitments and to serve as models to their communities. The Cornell Tradition also supports the development of fellows into well-rounded, productive members of society who, as alumni, will continue to support the program both financially and through active involvement with those fellows who follow in their footsteps.

As a consequence of this integrated design, Tradition fellows are exposed to the important role played by alumni and donors from the time of their initial acceptance into the program.

Fellows are chosen in two ways. All incoming freshmen and transfers who apply for financial aid are reviewed by a campuswide selection committee, and approximately 150 are selected each year. They are evaluated on a fourteen-point scale, which awards 0–5 points for work experience, 0–3 points for community service and extracurricular activities, 0–1 points for academic record, and 0–5 points for overall quality and potential. Analysis over the years indicates that the work component is the strongest indicator of whether a student is selected for the program. To continue as Tradition fellows, students must work at least 250 hours (200 hours for freshmen), participate in a minimum of 75 hours of community service or campus leadership activities, and maintain a minimum grade point average (GPA) of 2.3 each academic year. Upperclassmen may apply directly to the program and are evaluated in a competitive process, based on how well they meet or exceed the minimum Tradition requirements. Fellows are made aware of the importance of alumni support in a number of different ways. Many of the awards are named fellowships funded by individual donors, and fellows are strongly encouraged to write thank you letters to the donors to introduce themselves. The importance of donors and alumni to the success of the program is highlighted in a number of undergraduate publications. At reunions and a number of important campus events throughout the year, current fellows are given the opportunity to meet with alumni and donors in informal social situations. The Tradition Alumni Mentor Network allows fellows to contact alumni to discuss career plans, internship and job-shadowing opportunities, and related issues. The purpose of all these activities is to foster strong personal bonds among current fellows, the program, and its supporters.

In addition to providing financial benefits in the form of loan reduction, the Tradition sponsors a number of activities to encourage identification with and attachment to the program. The student advisory council organizes social activities and community service opportunities for fellows and offers proposals and feedback to the program staff. Cornell Commitment Leadership Emergence Assessment and Development, a program open to sophomore fellows, provides leadership training and support for fellows interested in taking leadership roles on campus and in the community. All first-time fellows participate in orientation and team-building activities to introduce them to the program and to one another. Current fellows also play a prominent role in recruitment through "phonathons," during which they contact students who have received admissions offers from the university and have been awarded Tradition fellowships.

A unique characteristic of the Cornell Tradition is the wide degree of freedom that fellows have in the way they structure their participation in the program. As long as they meet the minimum number of hours in the work and service-leadership categories and the minimum GPA, fellows are free to decide for themselves what type of jobs or activities in which to participate. The freedom to choose how to fulfill the requirements allows fellows to optimize their Tradition experience and helps explain the popularity of the program with the vast majority of fellows. According to survey research, 66 percent of current fellows rate their experience as excellent, and another 30 percent rate it as good.

The program staff fills an important role in assisting fellows by informing them of opportunities and encouraging them to pursue the options of greatest interest to them. The staff also works hard to maintain a personal relationship with the fellows. The staff members are available to offer assistance to fellows whether or not it involves an issue directly related to their participation in the program. The respect shown for the needs of individuals, the strong service orientation of the staff, and the personal nature of the relationships help connect fellows to the larger goals of the program. This reflects the integrated design of the Tradition.

The Tradition offers participants practical as well as less tangible rewards. For most participants, given their aid status and financial need, not working while attending Cornell is not an option. The Tradition program offers special recognition to working students who strive to be well-rounded individuals. Because the Tradition program offers summer internships and replaces expected summer saving with grants, the Tradition serves to "level the playing field" between working students and their wealthier peers by enabling fellows to take unpaid positions with nonprofit agencies. A number of alumni have commented that without the Tradition, they would not have been able to afford the cost of attending Cornell. The recognition, respect, and support the program offers for the traditional values of hard work, service and civic participation, and achievement resonate with those of its target population.

In a study comparing special-recognition programs at twenty-three colleges and universities, Scannell and Simpson (1996) drew a number of conclusions about the Cornell Tradition that relate to the strong ties Tradition alumni felt toward the program and their alma mater. Cornell was one of only three schools where participation in special-recognition programs strongly encouraged students to feel closer to their institution. Sixty-five percent of Tradition fellows shared this positive feeling toward their alma mater, compared with 25 to 40 percent of alumni at the other schools. Scannell and Simpson also found that there were statistically significant correlations between receiving a Tradition fellowship and acquiring such skills as adaptability and flexibility, improved self-confidence, and improved communication ability. Tradition participation also had a positive impact on current involvement in alumni activities.

In sum, the Cornell Tradition program provides an excellent example of strong institutional commitment to the creation of an integrated program that aims at achieving both long- and short-term goals.

The Study

The data consist of postgraduate surveys of all Cornell Tradition participants from the classes of 1990 and 1992, along with a matched control group of nonparticipants. The control group was sampled from the same graduating class as the Tradition group based on stratified random sampling on the basis of gender, ethnicity, college of enrollment at Cornell, and financial aid status. Alumni were surveyed three years after graduation during the winter-spring of 1993 and 1995. For the class of 1990, the response rate was 55 percent ($N = 132$) for fellows and 56 percent ($N = 134$) for the control group, yielding 266 responses. The response rate for the class of 1992 was 53 percent ($N = 71$) and 57 percent ($N = 79$) respectively, for 150 responses, giving us a total of 416 usable responses. To avoid any positive bias on the part of Tradition fellows toward the program, the surveys were conducted by a separate office, and no references were made to the Cornell Tradition. In addition to self-reported data from the alumni surveys, we also included historical institutional data from the university's registrar, financial aid, and alumni affairs systems.

Our primary interest in this study was whether participation in the Cornell Tradition program had a positive impact on postgraduate behaviors involving service to and financial support for the university and community. As a consequence, we employed a multivariate analysis using step-wise logistic regression. As this was a survey of recent alumni who had been financial aid recipients as undergraduates, we realized that it was unlikely that we would discover any major donors so soon after graduation. We were more interested in whether they were financial supporters or volunteers than in the amount of money or time donated. We reasoned that establishing a pattern of donating time and money as a recent graduate would yield a number of positive benefits in the future, when these alumni were more established and financially secure.

Two other factors also influenced our decision to choose logistic regression. First, as with previous studies, the large number of nondonors violated several underlying assumptions of ordinary least squares linear regression (OLS) when applied to the amount of alumni donations. In cases like these, the OLS model may adequately fit the donor's data but not the nondonor's (Mulugetta, Murphy, Saleh and Brewster, 1990). The other factor influencing our choice of logistic regression was a large number of categorical or dichotomous variables.

Each of the four alumni outcome dependent variables was tested, using an identical step-wise logistic regression procedure in which predictor variables were added in six blocks. This process is at the heart of the I-C-E-O model. Block one introduced our input variables. These consisted of background demographic data. In block two, we entered our key institutional commitment variable, participation or nonparticipation in the Cornell Tradition program. We hypothesized that this was the key environmental variable influencing the postgraduate outcomes we were measuring. Block three introduced our other undergraduate environmental variables—college (statutory or endowed; see Table 4.4), GPA, and extracurricular activities. Block four added postgraduate environmental variables, including employment and graduate school status. In block five, we included financial outcomes. We finished the process with three postgraduate attitudinal outcomes in block six. The postgraduate behavioral outcomes were the four dependent variables of participation in community service, charitable donations, participation in alumni activities, and donations to Cornell.

A simple descriptive analysis identified some statistically significant differences between Tradition participants and the control group. These differences suggest that the institutional commitment to achieving the goals outlined in the Cornell Tradition mission statement is having some measurable effect in altering both the college environment and postgraduate outcomes.

On input characteristics, the average parental income of Tradition participants was significantly lower than in the control group, \$41,476 versus \$53,139 ($t = -4.261, p > .01$). Gender and ethnicity were similar for the two groups. There were also some critical differences in undergraduate environmental variables. The college extracurricular activities of Tradition participants and nonparticipants are summarized in Table 4.1.

The most important differences between Tradition participants and nonparticipants are in the community service and the other service (religious organizations and other difficult-to-categorize groups) categories. This is consistent with the Tradition's goal of encouraging, not requiring, community service and citizenship. Tradition participants also had a higher mean GPA than nonparticipants, 3.1338 versus 3.0176 ($t = 2.782, p > .01$).

There was little difference between Tradition participants and nonparticipants on two of the major postgraduate environmental variables. Seventy-six percent of each group were employed, and one-quarter of each group had earned an advanced degree within three years of graduation. Tradition partic-

Table 4.1. Undergraduate Extracurricular Activities

Variable	Tradition	Control Group	Chi-Square	Significance
Athletics	27.1%	27.5%	.009	.504
Student groups	49.2%	56.1%	2.365	.074
Community service	42.1%	25.0%	15.857	.000
Greek	36.3%	34.0%	.265	.337
Political	9.6%	9.0%	.046	.477
Other groups	27.1%	18.9%	4.638	.020

ipants were, however, more likely than nonparticipants to be enrolled currently in a graduate degree program, 40 percent versus 32 percent ($p < .05$).

With the exception of undergraduate student loan debt, financial outcomes were similar for both groups. Sixteen percent earned under $20,000, 51 percent reported earnings of $20,000 to 49,999, and only 10 percent earned over $50,000. Twenty percent, almost all of whom were graduate students, reported no income. The status of undergraduate loans was also virtually identical for the two groups. Fifteen percent had paid off their loans, 51 percent were currently making payments, and 25 percent had yet to begin repayment or were in deferral. The major difference between Tradition participants and the control group was the amount of student debt. The average undergraduate student loan debt for Tradition alumni was $5,691 compared with $8,412 for the control group ($t = -6.329$, $p < .0001$). Not surprisingly, given the intentions of the program, participation in the Tradition had a significant impact on lowering overall student debt. As yearly wage income was virtually identical for the two groups, this should have the result, all things being equal, of raising the disposable income of the Tradition group.

The two groups were equally likely to say volunteer work for one's community was important. Tradition participants were significantly more likely than nonparticipants, however, to express a willingness to invest time and money in programs that would benefit the university and Cornell undergraduates. The results of the three outcome attitudinal variables are summarized in Table 4.2.

Finally, on the four dependent variables, there were some major differences as well. These are summarized in Table 4.3. While a higher percentage of Tradition participants engaged in all four postgraduate activities being observed, the differences in the community service and Cornell University donor categories were striking and statistically significant. In addition to having a higher percentage of donors, Tradition participants also had a much higher mean donation than nonparticipants, $128 versus $38 ($t = 3.269$, $p < .001$). This is interesting given that Tradition alumni came from families

Table 4.2. Attitudes Toward Alumni Involvement and Community Service: Four-Point Scale

Attitudinal Variable	Tradition	Control	Significance
Willingness to invest money in CU programs to help undergraduates get a start with their careers	3.5127	3.3388	.005
Willingness to invest time and energy in programs to benefit CU and undergraduates	2.7393	2.4703	.000
Belief in importance of devoting time and energy to volunteer activities to improve the quality of community life	2.9447	2.8529	.175

Note: CU = Cornell University

Table 4.3. Postgraduate Outcomes

Variable	Tradition	Control	Chi-Square	Significance
Community volunteer	62.6%	49.4%	8.528	.002
Charitable giver	77.2%	77.7%	.015	.494
CU volunteer	26.1%	22.5%	.807	.214
CU donor	49.2%	39.8%	4.342	.023

Note: CU = Cornell University

with significantly lower incomes than nonparticipants. The difference may reflect the lower undergraduate loan debt of Tradition alumni, the closer tie fellows feel to the university, or a combination of both factors.

The overall picture of the Tradition program that emerges from an examination of these descriptive statistics is a positive one. The Tradition appears to be successful in recognizing and rewarding students who value hard work as well as public service and participation. These characteristics seem to carry over into postgraduate outcomes, whereby Tradition fellows remain involved in community service and financial support for the university at a higher rate than the control group. In the following section, we employ logistic regression analysis in an attempt to isolate the factors that are responsible for these differences.

A brief description on how logistic regression works may help readers have a better understanding of our regression results. Logistic regression is the statistical method for estimating the impact of independent variables on the probability of an event occurrence that has a dichotomous value (Hosmer and Lemeshow, 1989), for example, whether an alumnus is a gift giver or not. $\pi(x)$ represents the logistic distribution of conditional mean of the dependent variable (Y) given certain independent variables (Xs).

$$\pi(x) = \frac{e^{\beta_0 + \beta_1 x_1 + \ldots + \beta_i x_i}}{1 + e^{\beta_0 + \beta_1 x_1 + \ldots + \beta_i x_i}}$$

A logit transformation of $\pi(x)$, which is denoted by $g(x)$, enables us to use the desirable properties of a linear regression model as $g(x)$ is linear in its parameters, which can be dichotomous as well as continuous.

$$g(x) = \ln \frac{\pi(x)}{1 - \pi(x)} = \beta_0 + \beta_1 x_1 + \ldots + \beta_i x_i$$

Similar to the interpretation of linear regression, a beta coefficient represents the change in the logit $g(x)$ for a change of one unit in the dependent variable x. Together with the coefficient, the odds ratio, denoted by φ or Exp (β), is also a useful measure in logistic regression to approximate how much more likely the outcome (the odds) will be among those with $x = 1$ (for example, Cornell Tradition fellows) than among those with $x = 0$ (for example, non-fellows). If β_i is positive, φ will be greater than 1, which indicates that the odds are increased. If β_i is negative, φ will be less than 1, meaning that the odds are decreased. If β_i is 0, then φ will be 0, indicating that the odds are left unchanged.

Table 4.4 presents the variables that were used in a stepwise logistic regression analysis of whether alumni made a financial contribution to the university. Variables that do not have names in the last column were omitted from the regression runs. Table 4.5 presents the results of the regressions. The significance of some demographic characteristics persists throughout the six steps. If the student is a female, a Caucasian, or an Asian, the odds of being a donor significantly increase. Within the need-based financial aid population, after controlling for ethnicity and gender, parental income did not make much difference in predicting whether the recipient would be a donor or not after graduation.

Undergraduate involvement in community service and other student activities (religious organizations, and so forth) moderately contributed to becoming an alumni donor. However, the involvement in specific activities (for example, athletics, student groups, Greek systems, or politics), GPA, and the college the student attended did not have a significant impact on alumni giving.

Among postgraduation variables, financial capability, which was measured by their income and employment status, seems to be a key factor in explaining postgraduation gift-giving behavior. This is not surprising. As the odds ratio indicates, the odds of making a donation to the university among alumni who are employed are approximately three times the odds among the unemployed. Similarly, having an income less than $20,000 reduces the probability of being a donor in comparison to those with incomes more than $20,000.

Postgraduation motivation, a twin concept along with financial capability (Volkwein and others, 1989), was measured by three questions on the alumni survey. The questions concerned (1) interest in investing money in Cornell's undergraduate programs, (2) interest in investing time and energy in those programs, and (3) assessment of the importance of investing time and energy in community volunteer activities. Surprisingly, the second measure turned out to be a significant predictor of alumni donor behavior rather than the first. Our correlation analysis (not presented here) indicates that the first question is correlated with employment status, and therefore the predictive power of the first attitudinal question becomes insignificant.

Participation in the Cornell Tradition program was inserted in the second block. The variable is significant at each step, indicating that the odds of becoming an alumni donor are almost one and a half times as great among program participants as the odds among the nonparticipants. This finding supports our hypothesis that in comparison to their peers, the Cornell Tradition participants to whom the institution had made a special commitment were more likely to grow into active alumni donors—the outcome the institution intended to produce.

Table 4.4. Variables and Values

Variable	Code-Value	Name in Table 4.5
Sex	0=Male 1=Female	Female
Ethnicity, underrepresented minority	Dropped dummy	
Ethnicity, white	0=Nonwhite 1=White	White
Ethnicity, Asian	0=Non-Asian 1=Asian	Asian
Parental income	Amount in $	Parental income
Tradition participation	0=No 1=Yes	Tradition student
College[a]	0=Statutory 1=Endowed	College
Grade point average		GPA
Varsity athletics	0=Nonparticipant 1=Participant	Athletics
Student extracurricular organization	0=Nonparticipant 1=Participant	Extracurricular
Community service organization	0=Nonparticipant 1=Participant	Community service
Sorority/fraternity member	0=Nonparticipant 1=Participant	Greek organization
Political/activist organization	0=Nonparticipant 1=Participant	Politics
Other groups or organizations	0=Nonparticipant 1=Participant	Other groups
Employment status	0=Unemployed 1=Employed	Employed
Graduate school status	0=Not attending 1=Attending	Graduate school
Graduate degree	0=No 1=Yes	Graduate degree
Income $0	Dropped dummy	
Income $20–$50K per year	0=No 1=Yes	I ($20K–$50K)
Income less than $20K per year	0=No 1=Yes	I (< $20K)
Income greater than $50K per year	0=No 1=Yes	I (> $50K)
Loan: deferred	Dropped dummy	
Loan: no loan	0=No 1=Yes	No loan
Loan: repaid loan	0=No 1=Yes	Repaid
Loan: currently repaying loan	0=No 1=Yes	Currently repaying
Loan: haven't started repayment	0=No 1=Yes	Not started
Undergraduate debt	Amount in $	Undergraduate debt
Invest $ in Cornell	4-point scale	Invest $

Table 4.4. *(continued)*

Variable	Code-Value	Name in Table 4.5
Invest time in Cornell	4-point scale	Invest time
Importance of volunteering	4-point scale	Community service importance
Dependent Variables		
Community service volunteer	0=No	
	1=Yes	
Charitable donations	0=No	
	1=Yes	
CU volunteer	0=No	
	1=Yes	
CU donor	0=No	
	1=Yes	

Note: CU = Cornell University

[a]Cornell University has seven undergraduate colleges. The Colleges of Architecture, Art, and Planning; Arts and Sciences; Engineering; and the Hotel School are private endowed colleges. The Colleges of Agriculture and Life Sciences; Human Ecology; and Industrial and Labor Relations are New York State land grant colleges, which are called statutory colleges.

One might argue that this finding may not be attributed to program participation. Rather, the predispositions to service of the Tradition fellows that were not included in our model and may or may not have been present in the control group might have produced this result. In other words, the consistent bias associated with the selection of the Cornell Tradition fellows (for example, their work experience and community involvement in high school) might have resulted in their active financial support for Cornell after graduation regardless of their participation in the program. This argument may be partially true. We lack adequate data on these input variables. As we stated previously, however, Tradition fellows are selected primarily on the basis of prior work experience, not community service. A current five-year postgraduate survey of the class of 1992 shows no statistically significant difference between Tradition fellows and the control group regarding whether they participated in community service in high school (77 percent of Tradition fellows participated versus 71 percent of the control group). Even here, however, we lack a measure of the quality of the volunteer effort or the amount of time spent in these activities. Given the weaknesses in our input data, we cannot conclusively rule out the argument that the differences in alumni outcomes that we are observing reflect selection bias. At the same time, it seems unlikely that these differences are solely the result of selection bias.

Even if we do partially attribute these differences to selection bias, one could argue that this is powerful evidence that Cornell has successfully identified the student's potential to be an effective alumni leader at the very beginning of the student's undergraduate career. Cornell also has successfully nurtured and molded the character of these students in the direction that it intended. The higher participation rate and average donation bode well for the

Table 4.5. Dependent Variable: Alumni Donations

	Step 1 Beta	Step 2 Beta	Step 3 Beta	Step 4 Beta	Step 5 Beta	Step 6 Beta	Odds/R Exp (β)
Constant	-1.38****	-1.81****	-1.05*	-1.66**	-1.24	-2.70**	
Female	0.32***	0.34*	0.41**	0.43**	0.39*	0.36*	1.43
White	1.08***	1.17****	1.17****	1.08***	1.19***	1.29*	3.62
Asian	0.95**	1.06***	1.06**	0.98**	1.07**	1.15*	3.17
Parental income	0.00	0.00	0.00	0.00	0.00	0.00	1.00
Tradition student		0.53***	0.56***	0.54***	0.47*	0.42*	1.52
College			0.10	0.08	0.10	0.11	1.12
GPA			-0.27	-0.19	-0.28	-0.26	0.77
Athletics			0.26	0.28	0.27	0.31	1.36
Extracurricular			-0.19	-0.16	-0.17	-0.19	0.82
Community service			0.05	0.10***	0.05	0.04*	1.04
Greek organization			-0.03	-0.02	-0.10	-0.15	0.86
Politics			-0.48*	-0.39**	-0.29	-0.29	0.75
Other groups			0.15*	0.18**	0.17	0.01*	1.01
Employed				0.56**	1.18**	1.19**	3.28
Graduate school				0.06	0.21	0.21	1.23
Graduate degree				-0.21	-0.10	-0.11	0.89
I ($20K–$50K)					-0.27	-0.29	0.75
I (< $20K)					-1.08*	-1.03*	0.36
I (> $50K)					-0.77	-0.92	0.40
No loan					0.38	0.61	1.85
Repaid					-0.14	0.02	1.02
Currently repaying					0.09	0.33	1.39
Not started					0.54	0.59	1.8
Undergraduate debt					-0.03	-0.03	0.97
Invest $						-0.07	0.93
Invest time						0.41*	1.50
Community service importance						0.14	1.15
2 Log L	563.03	556.42	549.90	544.56	530.30	518.94	
Negalkerke R²	.04	.06	.08	.10	.14	.17	
Model Chi-square	13.67	20.28	26.80	32.14	46.41	57.76	
Significance Level	***	****	***	***	***	****	

Note: Yes = 1, No = 2

*p < .1; **p < .05; ***p < .01; ****p < .001

future, as past donations are an excellent predictor of donations in the future (Lindahl and Winship, 1994).

A similar influence of the Cornell Tradition program can be on community service volunteering after graduation (tables available from authors). The program participation variable consistently showed a significant positive beta at each step of regression. According to the odds ratio, the odds of being a community volunteer increases by approximately 50 percent among the Tradition alumni compared to the non-Tradition alumni. Women are also significantly more likely than men to be involved in community service. This may be a reflection of the traditional affinity of women for nurturing roles. Other important indicators include having been involved in undergraduate student activities, particularly in community service and political organizations, and having motivation to make a financial contribution to Cornell. This may indicate a sense of social-obligation motivation on the part of community volunteers. Interestingly, if the student has obtained a graduate degree or is currently repaying undergraduate student loans, the odds of being involved in community service are substantially reduced.

The significant effect of the Tradition program on community volunteer service deserves special attention from a national policy perspective. At the Presidents' Summit on America's Future, held in Philadelphia in April 1997, leaders emphasized the importance of making the values of civic participation integral to the educational curriculum. They stressed the need to encourage two million more students and citizens to contribute volunteer services to improve our communities. The Cornell Tradition is a program that uniquely recognizes students' precollege work as well as community volunteering experience and encourages participants to continue to be involved in work, service, and citizenship during their undergraduate years and beyond. As the present study has shown, the Cornell Tradition's commitment to work, service, and citizenship recognizes and reinforces core values in the program participants, and as a result, many continue to serve their communities during their college years and after graduation.

The effect of the Cornell Tradition program is not so clear on the two remaining alumni behaviors. Participation in the Tradition program did not have much impact on the odds of a person becoming involved in alumni activities. Being a woman, being involved in student extracurricular groups, being a member of a sorority or fraternity, and having a higher GPA were significant in increasing the odds of becoming involved in alumni affairs. Having a smaller student loan and feeling strongly about making a financial contribution to undergraduate programs, as well as being involved in community service, were also good indicators. The study found that alumni who had earned a graduate degree within two years after graduation tend to shy away from Cornell's volunteering activities compared with their peers who had not. The impact of the Cornell Tradition program participation is rather insignificant after all other factors are taken into account. As noted, the participation rate for alumni volunteers was low for both groups—in the 22 to 26 percent range. Tradition staff thought that this might reflect, in part, a relative lack of opportunity for young alumni to have meaningful involvement in alumni affairs. As a result, they recently created the Tradition Alumni Mentor Network described previously. The positive alumni response to this opportunity is not reflected in the data we are reporting.

As for whether alumni have made charitable donations beyond their alma mater, again there is no significant difference between Tradition alumni and the control group. Undergraduate involvement in student activities as well as community service and attending one of the endowed (private) colleges had a negative impact on charitable giving. Only involvement in other undergraduate activities showed a positive impact on charitable-giving behavior, probably because involvement in religious activities is included in this category. Being in graduate school, earning incomes between $20,000 and $50,000, having completed loan repayments, and showing positive attitudes toward investing money and energy into undergraduate programs also increase the odds of being a charitable donor. Approximately three-quarters of the Tradition and the control group alumni reported making charitable donations.

Summary and Conclusion

This study has attempted to investigate what institutions can do to nurture or reinforce the values that will encourage undergraduates to support their institution financially or through their volunteer efforts after graduation. At the conceptual level, we have introduced the Input-Commitment-Environment-Output Model, in which institutional commitment plays a key role in producing intended student outcomes by creating and reinforcing particular environmental circumstances. Institutional commitment is defined as the degree to which the institution sustains its intention and acts to produce defined student outcomes by creating and reinforcing particular environmental circumstances.

We have tested this model by using Cornell University's data and examining the effect of participation in the Cornell Tradition, an undergraduate special-recognition program, on young alumni behavior. The study has found that efforts by the institution, through the creation of a comprehensive, integrated program that provides a sustained commitment to undergraduate students, can have a positive impact on the long-term behavior of alumni. The I-C-E-O model shows promise as a useful tool in understanding the differences between participants and nonparticipants in the Cornell Tradition program in postgraduate community service and alumni giving. This is true even when we control for participation in undergraduate community service groups and other activities and background variables.

As we have noted, it was not possible in this study to prove conclusively whether the differences we observed in alumni behavior were due primarily to program participation or whether they were the result of selection bias. The available evidence, however, suggests that participation in the Tradition program has a measurable impact on alumni behavior. Even if some selection bias is present, the Tradition is very successful in identifying and rewarding students who possess the type of qualities it wishes to reinforce and in creating and reinforcing their behavior in the desired direction. We are exploring these competing explanations in more depth in a study currently in process. In both cases, however, the results of the present study clearly indicate that participation in the Tradition program is an undergraduate activity that produces a statistically significant relationship with alumni giving and other postgraduate behaviors.

What makes a difference in nurturing active young alumni? Institutional commitment is the answer of the present study.

References

Astin, A. W. *Assessment for Excellence: The Philosophy and Practice of Assessment and Evaluation in Higher Education.* Old Tappan, N.J.: Macmillan, 1991.

Astin, A. W. *What Matters in College?* San Francisco: Jossey-Bass, 1993.

Brittingham, B. E., and Pezzulo, T. R. *The Campus Green: Fund Raising in Higher Education.* ASHE-ERIC Higher Education Report, no. 1. Washington, D.C.: School of Education and Human Development, George Washington University, 1990.

Connolly, M. S., and Blanchette, R. "Understanding and Predicting Alumni Giving Behavior." In J. A. Dunn Jr. (ed.), *Enhancing the Management of Fund Raising.* New Directions for Institutional Research, no. 51. San Francisco: Jossey-Bass, 1986.

Fitch, R. T. "Characteristics and Motivations of College Students Volunteering for Community Service." *Journal of College Student Personnel,* 1987, 28 (5), 424–431.

Gladieux, L. E., and Hauptman, A. M. *The College Aid Quandary: Access, Quality, and the Federal Role.* Washington, D.C.: Brookings Institution, 1995.

Gose, B. "Following Princeton Move, Yale Increases the Size of Its Student-Aid Packages." *Chronicle of Higher Education,* 1998, 44, A54.

Hauptman, A. M. *The Tuition Dilemma: Assessing New Ways to Pay for College.* Washington, D.C.: Brookings Institution, 1990.

Hosmer, D. W., and Lemeshow, S. *Applied Logistic Regression.* New York: Wiley, 1989.

Hubbell, L.W.L. "Tuition Discounting Is on the Rise." *Business Officer,* 1995, 28 (8), 27–31.

Lapovsky, L. "Tuition Discounting Continues to Climb." *Business Officer,* 1996, 29 (8), 20–25.

Lindahl, W. E., and Winship, C. "A Logit Model with Interactions for Predicting Major Gift Donations." *Research in Higher Education,* 1994, 35 (6), 729–743.

Mulugetta, Y., Murphy, S., Saleh, D., and Brewster, A. "Cultivating the Loyalty of Young Alumni to Their Alma Mater: The Success of the Cornell Tradition Program." Paper presented at the Seventeenth Annual Conference of the North East Association for Institutional Research, Albany, N.Y., October 1990.

Mulugetta, Y., Saleh, D., and Mulugetta, A. "Student Aid Issues at Private Institutions." In Richard A. Vorhees (ed.), *Researching Student Aid: Creating an Action Agenda.* Jossey-Bass: San Francisco, 1997.

Murphy, S., and Mulugetta, Y. "Making a Difference: The Cornell Tradition." *College Board Review,* 1994, 173, 22–24.

Scannell, J., and Simpson, K. *Shaping the College Experience Outside the Classroom.* Rochester, N.Y.: University of Rochester Press, 1996.

"Stanford Increases Financial Aid Following Princeton and Yale." *Chronicle of Higher Education,* 1998, 44, A8.

Stecklow, S. "Aid Policies to Change at Princeton." *Wall Street Journal,* Jan. 20, 1998, p. A3.

Volkwein, J. F., and others. "A Model of Alumni Gift Giving Behavior." Paper presented at the annual forum of the Association for Institutional Research, Baltimore, May 1989.

Young, P. S., and Fischer, N. M. "Identifying Undergraduate and Post-College Characteristics That May Affect Alumni Giving." Paper presented at the annual forum of the Association for Institutional Research, Albuquerque, May 1996.

YUKO MULUGETTA is director of research and planning analysis for admissions and financial aid at Cornell University.

SCOTT NASH is research associate for admissions and financial aid at Cornell University.

SUSAN H. MURPHY is vice president for student and academic services at Cornell University.

Comparative alumni research data can be used by individual institutions and entire sectors of higher education to study, improve, and promote themselves. A large multi-institutional alumni study in Pennsylvania provides one example of the methods and benefits of such research.

Using Comparative Alumni Data for Policy Analysis and Institutional Assessment

Michael D. McGuire, Jason P. Casey

Higher education in the United States is undergoing a critical scrutiny in the 1990s that is unprecedented in scope and passion. Parents, students, and government leaders alike are increasingly calling into question the value of a college degree. This scrutiny is fueled by at least two phenomena—the well-documented escalation of the costs of college attendance over the past two decades and concerns about the'employment prospects and even the employability of today's college graduates. Both of these drivers have received extensive and largely negative media coverage, some of which has included strikingly horrific anecdotal accounts of families whose lives have been derailed rather than enriched by higher education. On various occasions the media have described

College graduates who are reduced to living at home with their parents or working at fast-food restaurants (or both) for lack of more appropriate employment opportunities

Graduates whose student loan debts are so massive that they either select a career because of its income potential rather than their intrinsic interest in the subject or postpone marriage, child rearing, and home ownership because their student loan repayments have left them too impoverished to afford other important life pursuits

Parents who have had to make severe sacrifices in their own lifestyles (for example, selling the family house and other important family assets, or postponing retirement) to put their children through college

In addition to fanning the flames of consumer worry and anger, such reports have led to legislative action. Some states have imposed stringent funding restrictions and reporting requirements on colleges and universities. In Washington, the National Commission on the Cost of Higher Education issued a report in January 1998, urging greater cost containment and financial disclosure efforts on the part of postsecondary institutions (National Commission on the Cost of Higher Education, 1998).

Call for Accountability

Against this backdrop, the pressure on colleges and universities to maximize and demonstrate their effectiveness is at an all-time high. Because a college education is a lifelong investment with presumed dividends accruing for many years after graduation, it is logical to seek out compelling answers to the public's legitimate concerns through research on alumni. For years, many institutions have routinely conducted alumni surveys to gather information about their former students. Such research increases in value when it occurs in a comparative context, that is, when groups of institutions sharing key characteristics administer the same survey to the same alumni class(es). The advantages of comparative alumni research over isolated institutional studies are significant:

• By receiving comparable data about other institutions, the target institution can determine the degree to which its strengths and weaknesses are universal, and it can identify institutions that are ahead of or behind it on a given measure.

• The target institution, through follow-up contact with other institutions, can diagnose the causes and consequences of its shortcomings and develop strategies to remedy them.

• Although the identification of other institutions is typically forbidden or severely curtailed in comparative studies, the ability to make aggregate "better than" or "worse than" statements creates a valuable context in which senior management can understand the target institution's status. This information can then be used to establish optimal policies and practices on campus.

• In larger public policy discussions, multi-institutional data sets carry much greater weight than data from a single college or university, because they describe effects that are generalizable—within limits—rather than idiosyncratic.

Comparative alumni survey research is usually coordinated by a consortium with data-sharing capabilities, such as the Consortium on Financing Higher Education (COFHE), the Higher Education Data Sharing (HEDS) Consortium, and the Pennsylvania Independent College and University Research Center (PICURC). We believe that a variety of other organizations, including other state associations or state systems, denominational groups, and metropolitan area consortia, could produce valuable comparative data as well.

In 1996, PICURC undertook a study to examine the experiences five years after graduation of the 1990 baccalaureate graduates at forty-six independent colleges and universities in Pennsylvania. Funded by a grant from the Vira I.

Heinz Endowment, the PICURC study examined a number of key outcomes—postbaccalaureate employment, postbaccalaureate educational pursuits, social and personal development, satisfaction with undergraduate education, and undergraduate student loan borrowing and repayment trends. The findings were used to address the public policy concerns mentioned above and to fuel institutional self-study and improvement efforts.

PICURC Study: Sample and Procedures

One of the goals of the study design was to have as large and representative a sample of alumni, and as high a response rate, as possible within the control and resources of the investigators. Accordingly, a total of 11,108 members of the class of 1990 at forty-six independent colleges and universities in Pennsylvania were invited to participate in the study. This represented over one-third of the baccalaureate recipients at all independent colleges and universities in Pennsylvania that year. A four-page survey and cover letter were mailed to alumni in the spring of 1996. A follow-up survey was later sent to nonrespondents, and a sample of individuals who failed to respond to either of the mail waves were called and administered the survey by telephone. For additional details on the methodology and results of the study, including additional statistical analyses, confidence interval tables, and references, see McGuire and Casey (1997) and Pennsylvania Independent College and University Research Center (1997).

The overall response rate was 61 percent (6,811 completed surveys) with 42 percent ($N = 4,672$) of the original sample returning the survey by mail and 19 percent ($N = 2,139$) of the overall sample responding in follow-up telephone interviews.

For institutions with fewer than 360 graduates in the class, all graduates were surveyed. At institutions with more than 360 graduates, a random sample of 360 alumni were selected by stratifying the graduate population by gender and state of residence (Pennsylvania versus other) and assuring random selection of at least 90 graduates per cell whenever possible. Graduates living outside the United States were excluded due to the cost and difficulty of collecting data from them. Although necessary, this restriction was unfortunate because it precluded measuring the postbaccalaureate outcomes of graduates often engaged in especially interesting, useful, or lucrative ventures. Finally, PICURC weighted responses by the inverse of the institutional response rate to reflect proportionately the size of the entire alumni sample.

Survey Instrument and Supplemental Data

The alumni questionnaire was intended to address a broad range of institutional and public policy concerns and consisted of seven parts:

Designation of activities (employment, postbaccalaureate education, and volunteer work) in the fall of 1990 and the fall of 1995

Specific information on postbaccalaureate educational pursuits, including the
  year, degree, field, institution, and state of each degree pursued, as well as
  plans for future educational attainment

Specific information on experiences at two-year colleges while, or prior to,
  receiving a bachelor's degree

Specific information on the respondents' employment status in 1995, including occupation and job title, employer activity/type of business, location,
  salary and fringe benefits, longevity, and supervisory responsibility, for both
  primary and secondary employment, if appropriate

Evaluations of respondents' satisfaction with their undergraduate education
  and of the effectiveness and relevance of undergraduate skill development
  in each of eight areas

Indebtedness from student loans for both undergraduate and graduate education

Demographic characteristics of alumni, including marital and parental status;
  family income and home ownership; amount of unpaid volunteer service
  performed for community or religious organizations; and highest educational
  attainment of the respondents' mother, father, and spouse, as appropriate

In addition to the data collected on the survey itself, PICURC obtained
background information for a subset of respondents from the undergraduate
institutions. These supplemental data, which were merged with unit-record
survey responses, included gender, ethnicity, age, citizenship, major, undergraduate matriculation status (full-time versus part-time, first-time versus
transfer), undergraduate GPA and rank in class, precollegiate Scholastic Assessment Test (SAT) scores, and annual fund-giving status. PICURC kept all data,
both survey responses and background information, strictly confidential at all
times.

Testing for Sample Bias

The data were examined for four possible sources of sampling bias—differences between the participating and nonparticipating independent colleges and
universities of Pennsylvania (institutional-sample bias), differences between the
original sample and the respondent pool (respondent bias), differences between
paper and phone survey respondents (administration-type bias), and differences
between the respondents for whom PICURC did or did not receive secondary
data from their institutions (secondary-data bias).

Regarding institutional-sample bias, the participating colleges and universities represented all of the major institution types in Pennsylvania but
excluded the four most selective independent institutions in the state. This suggests that the results, if anything, may underestimate positive outcomes.
Regarding response bias, the respondent pool ended up with disproportionately more women (61 percent) than the sample pool (58 percent) due to a
predictably higher response rate among female respondents (64 percent ver-

sus a 57 percent response rate for males). This difference did not appear to be significant, and in any event, the analyses included separate data tables for men and women. There were no other background variables on which PICURC received information from enough institutions to compare the respondent and nonrespondent pools conclusively. The large response variability observed on most of the survey questions suggests that respondents do not appear to have come disproportionately from one part of the population.

Regarding administration-type bias, small differences existed between paper and phone survey respondents on a number of variables. For example, there were proportionately more males in the phone sample, consistent with their lower response rate on the paper survey—only those who did not return the paper survey were given the opportunity to complete the survey by phone. These differences did not appear to introduce any systematic bias to the data (for example, the phone survey respondents were not significantly different in terms of employment status or satisfaction with their undergraduate education). This served also as a partial check on potential social desirability effects in the phone sample, as those who responded to the mail survey did not differ systematically from those who refused to complete it (mail nonrespondents) but were available and willing to participate over the phone. Finally, there were no consistent differences between respondents whose institutions provided supplemental data and those for whom institutionally supplied data were unavailable.

In summary, our tests failed to find evidence of response bias. That is not to say that there was no possibility of bias, but simply that no gross effects were detected.

How Graduates Fared: Aggregate Findings

There were eleven key outcomes of the study. This section discusses the major findings. (We should point out prior to reporting the findings that we have not reported the results of statistical significance tests on the data because the power of such tests, inflated by the large sample size, yielded differences that were statistically significant but trivial in magnitude. The term *significant* used here reflects a subjective evaluation of the size and importance of perceived effects, not the results of statistical tests.)

   Outcome One: Postbaccalaureate Employment Rates, 1990 and 1995. In the fall immediately after graduation, 70 percent of the members of the class of 1990 reported being employed full-time, 14 percent were employed part-time, 2 percent were unemployed by choice, and 6 percent were unemployed and seeking employment. Note that these are duplicated counts based on self-reports (that is, graduates could report being employed both full-time and part-time if they held two jobs). The numbers do not add to 100 percent because some people were still enrolled in advanced degree programs (see Outcome Four). Five years later, in the fall of 1995, 84 percent reported being employed full-time, 9 percent were employed part-time, 4 percent were unemployed by choice, and

2 percent were unemployed and seeking employment. Men were more likely than women to be employed full-time in 1995, whereas women were more likely than men to be unemployed by choice (7 percent versus 1 percent).

Outcome Two: Salary and Fringe Benefits. On average, graduates who were employed full-time earned about $37,664 annually, a figure that increased or decreased about $500 depending on how conservatively one defines full-time employment. (Our base definition—at least thirty-one hours per week for at least thirty-seven weeks of the year—was a conservative one, which if anything underestimated actual mean salary.) Males earned more than females, with a gender gap of about $3,900. However, this gender gap was much narrower for holders of master's, doctoral, law, and medical degrees ($1,800) than for holders of baccalaureate degrees only ($4,400).

Ninety-three percent of respondents lived in a household with one (36 percent) or two (57 percent) wage earners. Forty-one percent of graduates lived in households with gross incomes of $60,000 or higher, and 10 percent enjoyed family incomes of more than $100,000. Only 6 percent of graduates lived in households with gross income of less than $20,000. See Figure 5.1.

The majority of those employed full-time enjoyed a range of fringe benefits, including health care (92 percent) paid vacation (91 percent), and retirement-pension plans (65 percent), with no significant gender differences for those benefits.

Outcome Three: Supervisory Experience. Approximately 67 percent of graduates who were employed full-time had supervisory responsibility in their primary job. Thirty-eight percent supervised one to five people, 20 percent supervised six to twenty people, and 10 percent supervised more than twenty people. Among full-time employees, men were slightly more likely than

Figure 5.1. Gross Family Income

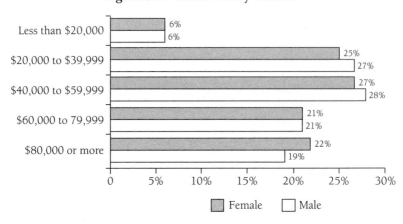

Note: Percentages add up to 101 due to rounding.

women to work more than forty hours per week and to supervise more than five people.

Outcome Four: Rates of Postbaccalaureate Educational Attainment. More than one-fourth (26 percent) of graduates had earned a postbaccalaureate degree by the spring of 1996, and 12 percent were in the process of completing degrees. About one in five graduates (19 percent) indicated that they had no educational plans beyond the bachelor's degree. The most common advanced degrees were master's degrees. Large numbers of graduates also pursued further education outside traditional degree programs, including courses offered through their employer (60 percent), training courses offered by another company (23 percent), and credit courses offered by a four-year college or university (23 percent). Overall, 88 percent of the class of 1990 had started a postbaccalaureate degree, completed another degree, or completed other training by 1995.

Outcome Five: Social and Personal Development. Fifty-five percent of graduates were married at the time of the survey; 41 percent were single and had never married; and 4 percent were divorced, separated, or widowed. Twenty-seven percent reported first meeting their spouse while in college, with males (32 percent) more likely than females (24 percent) to have done so. Seventy percent of graduates reported that their spouse had a bachelor's degree or higher, with males' spouses more likely than females' spouses to have a bachelor's degree or higher (75 percent versus 67 percent). Twenty-eight percent of graduates reported being the legal guardian of at least one child, and almost half of these had two or more children.

Outcome Six: Home Ownership. Fifty-one percent of graduates owned their own home at the time of the survey. Overall, females were more likely than men to own homes (53 percent versus 48). This trend was consistent at all income levels and across all marital statuses. Also, there was a strong correlation between institutional tuition and home ownership—more graduates of institutions with lower tuition owned their own homes than did graduates from high-tuition institutions. However, the fact that neither total student loan volume nor residual loan debt was related to home ownership makes it unclear whether the correlation with tuition level is related to personal wealth, lifestyle (such as urban dwellers living in apartments), or some other underlying characteristic of alumni.

Outcome Seven: Volunteerism. Fifty-four percent of graduates indicated that they had performed some unpaid volunteer service in 1995 for community, religious, or other nonprofit organizations. Forty-six percent reported performing an average of one to five hours of volunteer service per week, 4 percent volunteered six to ten hours per week, and 3 percent performed eleven or more hours of community service per week.

Full-time employees volunteered an average of one-half hour per week more than graduates who were not employed full-time. No statistically significant differences were observed between males and females or between graduates of religiously affiliated (whether aggregated or separated into Catholic and Protestant) versus nonsectarian institutions. Admission rate of the institution was negatively related to weekly hours volunteered—graduates of more selective institutions volunteered more, on average, than did graduates of less selective institutions. These findings should not be overinterpreted in the absence of additional research, as the magnitude of the differences was small.

Outcome Eight: Annual Fund Giving. Sixty-two percent of sampled alumni for whom data were available have given to their alma mater's annual fund at least once since graduation. Only student loan indebtedness was correlated with donating to the institution—as debt level increased, the likelihood of making a charitable contribution decreased. Gender, household income, and institutional characteristics (including selectivity and religious affiliation) were not significantly correlated with giving.

Outcome Nine: Time to Degree. Mean time to degree at the degree-granting institution was 3.9 years. Note that this is not a graduation rate, as it "counts backward" to initial matriculation for a graduating cohort rather than counting forward to graduation for an entering cohort. Full-time attendees who had previously attended a two-year college took fewer years (mean = 3.4) at the baccalaureate-granting institution to earn their degree. No statistically significant difference between males and females in time to degree was observed.

Outcome Ten: Satisfaction with Undergraduate Education. Alumni were asked to indicate their level of satisfaction with their undergraduate educational experience on three dimensions—academic experience, social experience, and overall experience. In general, graduates exhibited high levels of satisfaction with all dimensions. The academic experience (96 percent satisfied or very satisfied) was regarded somewhat more positively than social experience (90 percent), but even on the latter dimension, there was relatively little dissatisfaction expressed. Ninety-six percent were satisfied or very satisfied with their overall undergraduate experience. There were no differences of more than a single percentage point on any of these measures between men and women.

More than half of the respondents indicated that they were at least satisfied with their undergraduate experience, and significant numbers—44 percent for academic experience, 41 percent for overall experience, and 38 percent for social experience—indicated that they were very satisfied. In other words, many graduates expressed not simply marginal but extreme satisfaction with their undergraduate institutions. Females were somewhat more likely than males (47 percent versus 39 percent) to be very satisfied with their academic experience but about as likely to be very satisfied with their social experience.

Positive recollections of college were also reflected on two other items, which asked alumni if they had recommended their undergraduate institution to another person in the past five years and if they would encourage another person with similar skills and interests to attend that institution. The vast majority of graduates, 79 percent and 86 percent respectively, responded affirmatively to these two questions.

Outcome Eleven: Student Loan Indebtedness. Several items on the survey dealt with both undergraduate and postbaccalaureate student loans and residual indebtedness. Overall, 59 percent of respondents reported participating in student loan programs for their undergraduate education; 16 percent of respondents, or 33 percent of those for whom the question was applicable, had borrowed money for graduate-professional school. There were no significant gender differences in the tendency to take out student loans.

The average (median) amount borrowed for undergraduate education was $11,000, of which 44 percent was still owed at the time of the survey. Similarly, the median amount borrowed for postbaccalaureate education was $15,000, of which 84 percent was still owed at the time of the survey. Not surprisingly, the residual indebtedness for graduate-professional school was significantly larger than that for undergraduate loans.

On average, men appear to have borrowed more than women at both the undergraduate ($2,000 more) and graduate ($3,000 more) levels, which may be a function of different financial circumstances, postbaccalaureate educational goals, or both. Approximately 10 percent of respondents had taken out both undergraduate and graduate student loans, with an average total amount borrowed of $29,000.

The average student loan levels for graduates from families in the middle socioeconomic strata, as measured by parental educational attainment, were somewhat higher than for graduates in the lowest and highest socioeconomic categories. This makes sense in purely economic terms: students from the wealthiest backgrounds do not need to borrow as much money to pay for college, and those from the least wealthy backgrounds may be either disinclined or ineligible to borrow as much. These data provide evidence of the financial stress felt by many middle-income individuals and families who are required to borrow more heavily than other socioeconomic groups to achieve their educational goals.

Disaggregated Findings: Subgroup Profiles

The aggregate findings, supplemented by comparisons of groups defined by gender, household income, and type of institution, provide many important insights into the postcollegiate lives of the class of 1990. A second level of analysis looks at specific subgroups that are important for public policy. Two such groupings discussed below are based on undergraduate academic major and migration patterns (that is, which states undergraduates came from and where they go after graduation). Other groups that would have important policy implications are people who have student loan debt, low-income students, and students from minority groups.

Academic Major Profiles. The summary table (Table 5.1) lists the academic fields that had at least one hundred majors and some of the key outcomes for graduates in each field. By far the most popular majors were in business and management, with more than twice as many majors (N = 1,598) as

Table 5.1. Academic Major Profiles

Academic Field	Percentage Remaining in Pennsylvania	Percentage Employed Full-Time	Percentage Encouraging Others to Attend	Average Primary Occupation Salary ($)	Median Total Educational Loans ($)	N
Business, management	60	82	86	38,071	12,000	1,598
Communications, media	50	79	82	33,657	10,000	296
Computer science	71	90	86	42,653	12,000	229
Design, architecture	39	64	77	30,640	12,093	132
Education	60	64	85	28,090	12,000	697
Engineering	54	88	86	45,597	12,770	431
Fine and performing arts	46	54	80	29,171	13,000	155
Humanities	46	69	77	31,996	14,000	619
Mathematics	59	77	84	37,447	12,000	225
Medicine	62	73	92	46,692	20,000	216
Other health field	66	77	89	44,335	14,000	558
Natural sciences	50	79	84	34,684	15,000	538
Public policy, government	41	78	84	37,137	16,000	174
Social sciences	55	73	85	31,676	13,000	651
Social work	70	69	88	28,495	13,000	102

the second most popular major, education (N = 697). There were marked differences across fields on each measure, especially average salary, which ranged from $28,090 (education) to $46,692 (medicine). Indebtedness from student loans also varied considerably by undergraduate major, ranging from $10,000 (communications and media) to $20,000 (medicine). Full-time employment rates were highest for those majoring in computer science (90 percent) and engineering (88 percent) and lowest for fine and performing arts majors (54 percent).

Analysis of the undergraduate academic fields of the class of 1990 revealed common academic backgrounds among graduates within professional areas. Although most early childhood teachers (78 percent) majored in education in college, by contrast, secondary teachers came from a wider variety of academic backgrounds, including education (37 percent), humanities (23 percent), natural sciences (14 percent), and mathematics (11 percent). Like early childhood education, other occupations that tended to draw alumni from one or two majors were engineering (engineering majors = 74 percent), physicians (natural sciences = 69 percent), and accounting and finance (business or management = 62 percent). Like secondary teachers, lawyers came from a variety of academic majors including humanities (24 percent), public policy or government (19 percent), business or management (16 percent), social sciences (12 percent), and prelaw (7 percent).

Migration Patterns. An important public policy issue addressed in the PICURC study was the extent to which private colleges and universities attract capable students to Pennsylvania from other states, and the extent to which both those "imported" students and those native to Pennsylvania remain in the Commonwealth after college to participate in the labor force or advanced educational settings. The results indicated that two-thirds (67 percent) of the graduates surveyed were Pennsylvania residents before pursuing their undergraduate studies here. Women were slightly more likely than men (68 percent versus 64 percent) to have come from Pennsylvania. New Jersey (12 percent) was the next most common state of origin.

Of those originally from Pennsylvania, 74 percent were still living in the state in 1996, whereas 26 percent had moved to another state. Of those who came to Pennsylvania from other states for their undergraduate studies, 19 percent were still living here in 1996. Altogether, 59 percent of graduates were residing in Pennsylvania at the time of the survey, regardless of their state of origin. New Jersey (10 percent) was the second most frequent state of residence for graduates of Pennsylvania's private institutions five years after college.

On average, the profile of graduates from out of state was strongly traditional (that is, they typically enrolled full-time and resided on campus during college, and their parents and current spouses had relatively high levels of education). They were more likely than native Pennsylvanians to have started as first-year students in their degree-granting institutions, to be unmarried, and to be lifelong high achievers (that is, to earn higher salaries, complete more graduate and professional degrees, have higher class ranks in college and higher SAT scores before college, and so forth). Native Pennsylvanians included a more diverse mixture of graduates, with traditional and nontraditional attendance patterns, different socioeconomic backgrounds, and a variety of achievements reflected in later outcomes.

It is of interest that graduates who had come to Pennsylvania from another state had significantly higher SAT scores (approximately 40 points higher on verbal and 35 points higher on math) than natives. Students who came to Pennsylvania from another state and were living in Pennsylvania at the time of the survey had the highest SAT scores of all. This group also had higher average academic standings (or ranks) in their college graduating class, compared to native Pennsylvanians and to students originally from other states who were not living in Pennsylvania at the time of the survey. The lowest average class ranks were observed for both the latter group and Pennsylvania natives who were not living in Pennsylvania at the time of the survey. Though intriguing—and suggestive that students with higher SAT scores may possess the necessary self-confidence to attend college farther away from home and to settle in the area afterward—these findings should be considered exploratory, as not all institutions were able to provide SAT and class rank data on their graduates. Nevertheless, the PICURC institutions do appear to be importers of high achievers for the state, an important public policy consideration.

One way to summarize migration patterns is to examine original (precollege) and current (at time of survey) residence of graduates by region of the United States. Three generalizations emerged from this analysis:

Most graduates (69 percent) were residing in their region of origin five years after college.

Most of the students who graduated from a private institution in Pennsylvania originally came from either Pennsylvania (67 percent) or another state in the middle-Atlantic region (24 percent).

Although most graduates were living in Pennsylvania in 1996, of those originally from Pennsylvania who did not reside here at the time of the survey, most had moved elsewhere in the middle-Atlantic region (35 percent) or the southeast region (27 percent). This finding is consistent with regional population growth and economic opportunity trends in recent years.

Finally, for every type of postbaccalaureate degree achieved or pursued by graduates, Pennsylvania was the primary location of the graduate and professional schools, followed by other middle-Atlantic states.

Disaggregated Findings: Institutional Comparisons

As noted above, one of the best institutional uses of alumni research data involves comparisons of one institution with some or all of the other institutions in the sample, either individually or at some intermediate level of aggregation. Often in studies coordinated by consortia, participating institutions can select a subset of the other institutions (that is, those that are of greatest similarity in mission, size, market overlap, and so forth) and compare their own alumni survey findings with those of the comparison group. Another approach is to examine one institution's findings relative to the entire sample of institutions singly. Confidentiality agreements usually prevent the identification of individual comparison institutions.

The following figures illustrate how an individual institution (Institution A) can use comparative data to gain a better understanding of its alumni outcomes. In Figure 5.2, Institution A and all other participating Baccalaureate II colleges are displayed for three standardized financial outcome measures—average salary, average student loan indebtedness, and percent owning their own home. Institution A (represented by a triangle) fell between the twenty-fifth and seventy-fifth percentile on all measures; its graduates were below the median salary, above the median indebtedness, and above the median home ownership rate. On the surface, the relatively low average salaries and high average debt of Institution A's graduates do not seem to have deterred home ownership. These data should be interpreted cautiously because financial outcomes are correlated with occupation and undergraduate major, and there were marked differences across institutions on the latter, with some institutions graduating a higher share of their students in fields that are more likely

Figure 5.2. Institutional Comparisons

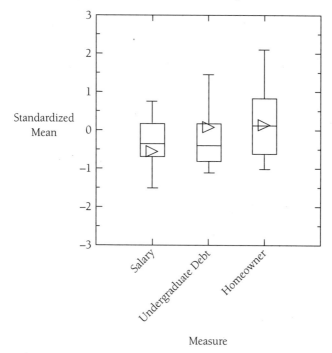

Measure

to lead to higher-paying occupations. A more focused variation on this analysis would be to conduct separate comparisons for alumni in the same field of work or study, although small subsample sizes would limit the number of fields for which reliable comparisons could be performed.

Figure 5.3 displays satisfaction with undergraduate academic and social experiences for all forty-six institutions in the study. (Each institution is represented by a symbol in the scatterplot.) Satisfaction in this analysis is defined as the percentage of graduates who indicated that they were very satisfied with the given experience. Overall, institutional satisfaction ratings ranged from 28 percent to 64 percent for academic experience and from 19 percent to 51 percent for social experience. (Keep in mind that about 20 percent of respondents would be expected to select a given option on a five-point scale if they responded randomly.) On a global level, graduates of all institutions were fairly satisfied. As indicated by the normal distributions of these measures (see the axes in Figure 5.3) and the scatterplot itself, no single institution stood out as highly aberrant. However, those institutions in the lower-left quadrant were by definition below average on both academic and social satisfaction. Furthermore, the two institutions with the lowest social satisfaction ratings had only average academic satisfaction ratings. These institutions, and any others who

Figure 5.3. Distributions of Academic and Social Satisfaction

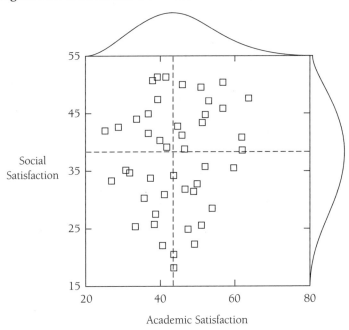

deem their relative position on the chart to be unsatisfactory, may profit from more detailed diagnostic analyses to try to pinpoint why their ratings were lower than they might have wished or expected. For example, multiple regression analysis of institutional data could be run with satisfaction as the dependent variable and items such as average salary and student loan debt as independent variables. Due to the confidentiality agreements of the PICURC data, such an analysis would have to be conducted by the project sta ⌐ rather than the participating institutions.

Institutional Uses of the PICURC Study

Institutions that participated in the study received three reports—detailed institution-specific tables of their own alumni's responses; an aggregate report with complete analyses for the entire sample of alumni; and an eight-page, four-color advocacy piece that featured highlights from the overall study. Due to resource and confidentiality constraints, customized comparative data files could not be prepared for each participating institution's own analyses.

The various reports were used in different ways by different departments on the individual campuses. The differences were typically influenced by the intended audience. Those doing internal presentations (for example, institutional researchers) focused on their own institutional data, with excerpts from the aggregate study included for context. For admissions, public relations, and development officers, who had a primarily external audience, the more colorful advocacy document was used almost exclusively.

Admissions personnel used the advocacy piece in various ways. One liberal arts college sent copies to selected segments of its admitted student pool as a final "yield" piece to increase the enrollment of admitted applicants by emphasizing the lasting value of an independent college education. Another institution used the advocacy piece in presentations to admissions counselors, as well as in interviews and telephone conversations with prospective students and their parents. This institution's representative felt that the career outcomes data were particularly useful in addressing some parents' concerns about the quality of a private college education. Yet another institution used the occupation and employment information to alter its characterization of its graduates: the information gave them a critical insight (that had previously been lacking) into their alumni's careers.

One telling indicator of the usefulness of this study is that most participating institutions are interested in repeating it periodically.

As noted above, the original study's cost was underwritten by generous grant funding. The participating institutions, as well as many of the institutions that did not participate in the current study, have indicated a willingness to finance another similar study themselves. Institutions have also expressed an interest in a ten-year follow-up study of the class of 1990.

Interpreting College Outcomes Data

The findings of the PICURC Alumni Survey, which achieved a high response rate with a relatively large sample of alumni from almost four dozen independent colleges and universities in Pennsylvania, revealed largely positive outcomes for the class of 1990.

The observed unemployment rate was lower than the state average, and the mean salary for full-time employees was higher than the state average after controlling for age, gender, and educational attainment. Combined with data on supervisory responsibility and fringe benefit packages, the results suggest a successful entry of most graduates into the labor force and onto career tracks. They also confirmed the continued existence of a gender gap in average salary, which was most pronounced among those who did not hold postbaccalaureate degrees.

One robust finding of this study is that the baccalaureate is not perceived to be a terminal degree. In addition to the many members of the class of 1990 who had already earned an advanced degree at the time of the survey, others either had a degree in progress or had plans to earn a graduate degree eventually, and still others had undertaken nondegree training and coursework. Increasingly, advanced training and education are necessary for career advancement in most fields of endeavor. The sheer intellectual stimulation of postbaccalaureate coursework, even when not in pursuit of an advanced degree, is probably a motivation of some graduates.

In addition to being employed or enrolled in graduate school (or both), respondents to the survey seem to be engaged productively as consumers, volunteers, taxpayers, spouses, and parents. Salaries and gross family incomes suggest that most graduates are earning very respectable livings and supporting the economies and tax base of the communities and states in which they live. The majority own their own home five years after graduating from college and participate in fringe benefits packages at work, another indicator of financial stability. Volunteer activity is a positive social indicator in which a majority of respondents had engaged recently. Notably, the graduates who were most involved in volunteer activity were those who were also employed full-time. Rather than focusing exclusively on their careers, many graduates find time to contribute to their communities in other important ways that are not always reflected in narrowly focused economic and labor market statistics.

The vast majority of graduates in the sample completed their baccalaureate in four years or less at the degree-granting institution. Although this is not a graduation rate, it is one piece of evidence suggesting efficient matriculation-to-degree attainment. Even more noteworthy than time to degree were respondents' evaluations of their undergraduate education. Five years after graduation, with many different intervening experiences, former students were asked to rate their satisfaction. Almost all were satisfied and had recommended or would recommend their alma mater to others. When all was said and done, with the immediate postbaccalaureate adjustments behind them, graduates gave their undergraduate experience an overwhelmingly positive grade.

Repayment of student loans is one economic reality that many college graduates have to face. The majority of survey respondents from the class of 1990 took out loans to finance their undergraduate education. It is noteworthy that those who completed their degrees over longer periods borrowed less, on average, than those whose time to degree was shorter. This makes sense in terms of eligibility for loans and total amount to be borrowed—those who attend full-time can be expected to finish more quickly but also to accumulate more student debt. Similarly, those who had attended a two-year institution prior to entering the four-year institution for completion of the baccalaureate were no less likely to borrow money, but they did accrue a smaller debt than those who had not attended a two-year institution. Finally, though there is no gender gap in borrowing patterns (that is, the proportions of females and males borrowing to finance their education were about the same), females tended to take out smaller loans than males did. It is clear that the borrowing habits of successful students is a complex dynamic, and that attempts to describe indebtedness in oversimplified or "worst case" terms will produce deceptive impressions.

Policy Implications

Findings from the PICURC Alumni Survey suggest that higher education is a sound investment, enabling the majority of its beneficiaries to embark on important life goals—worthwhile careers, a relatively high standard of living, and the pursuit of personal fulfillment for themselves and others through involvement in family and community life. One obvious public policy implication is that the opportunity to participate in this success story can and should be made available to as many citizens as possible. Funding and other mechanisms of preparation and access should therefore be expanded, ensuring both the financial and cognitive means to complete a bachelor's degree.

A second policy implication involves the dissemination of accurate information about graduates' life outcomes to prospective students and their families and to the public at large. Alarmist anecdotal accounts of graduates who are failing miserably at life after college are at best nonrepresentative of the vast majority of alumni. Unfortunately, the old adage that "good news doesn't sell" is as true for higher education as it is for other sectors of our society. To the extent that higher education cannot rely on the media automatically to offer a balanced accounting of the actual outcomes of college completion, it must persist in getting that message out. Broad-based and methodologically sound alumni research is perhaps the most credible mechanism for accomplishing this.

A third public policy implication stems from the second and has to do with unrealistic expectations of immediate postbaccalaureate gratification. Most alumni did not step into their dream job right after graduation. In reality, there is a predictable adjustment period during which additional graduate or professional education is undertaken, or entry-level jobs that permit the gaining of experience necessary for career advancement are performed. A bachelor's degree is not a guarantee of career success, and the first postbaccalaureate steps are almost never highly lucrative ones. One of the goals of disseminating accurate information about college outcomes should be to establish realistic expectations on the part of prospective students and their families. The PICURC study found widespread, significant progress toward lifetime career and personal fulfillment only five years after graduation. Realistic expectations will alleviate anxiety that may develop when first jobs after college do not produce the immediate financial returns some parents might have desired. Yes, college is expensive and requires financial sacrifice on the part of students and families. But when seen as a lifelong investment of approximately sixty years duration on average, the amortization schedule is both feasible and ultimately worthwhile.

Further Research

Additional research is needed to replicate and expand on the findings of the PICURC study. Some of the research has already been performed in one setting or another, in which case synthesis and dissemination are needed more than original research. Six areas of further inquiry are as follows:

• The PICURC study focused primarily on the outcomes of traditional students. What are the outcomes of nontraditional students, who constitute a significant percentage of college enrollments?

• The PICURC study also concentrated on the outcomes of a single cohort of graduates from independent colleges and universities in Pennsylvania. Will similar outcomes be observed with graduates from other cohorts, from public institutions, and from other states?

• Specifically, the class of 1990 reported a modest and manageable student loan burden. Can the same be said of later graduating cohorts who continue to borrow increasing amounts to finance their education?

• The PICURC study examined a "snapshot" of outcomes five years after college. What were the paths or processes that led graduates to their current stage of career development? How many and what types of intervening jobs and experiences occurred between graduation and one's present situation? Additional information might help students develop more realistic plans and expectations for how their own lives might progress after college, and it might give faculty and career guidance professionals better insights for understanding the marketplace and advising future student cohorts.

• The five-year snapshot was illuminative, but what are the outcomes ten, twenty, or more years out? Longer-term alumni surveys have already been performed by individual institutions and consortia. A similar multi-institutional study involving a diverse group of colleges and universities, as well as a synthesis of the research that has already been performed, would add even more texture to the argument that higher education should be viewed as a long-term investment rather than a short-term service or commodity.

• What are the later life outcomes of those who never attend college, or who start but do not persist to graduation? Some information exists, primarily of an economic nature, that demonstrates generally superior outcomes for college graduates (for example, Pennsylvania Independent College and University Research Center, 1995). It would be illuminating to use a standard survey technique to assess all of the outcome measures in the present study for members of the same age cohort regardless of whether they attended or graduated from college. Again, some information already exists (for example, the national High School and Beyond studies), although more is needed.

The present study suggests that popular doom-and-gloom predictions regarding the employability, economic stress, and overall success of recent college graduates are not borne out by systematic observation of a large alumni sample. On the contrary, most graduates are gainfully employed in positions of responsibility, well along in their repayment of student loans, active in their family and community lives, and highly satisfied with their undergraduate experiences. In many ways, these are some of the most important criteria by which to judge the efficacy of colleges and universities. All stakeholders in the higher education community—including faculty, admissions, and advancement leaders—need to increase their efforts to make this case with the evidence at hand.

References

McGuire, M. D., and Casey, J. P. "A Multi-Institutional Survey of Labor Market Outcomes: One Measure of Post-Baccalaureate Success That Matters." Paper presented at the annual forum of the Association for Institutional Research, Orlando, May 1997.

National Commission on the Cost of Higher Education. *Straight Talk About College Costs and Prices.* Washington, D.C.: American Institutes for Research, 1998.

Pennsylvania Independent College and University Research Center. *Higher Education Participation: The Key to Achieving a Commonwealth of Opportunity.* Harrisburg: Pennsylvania Independent College and University Research Center, 1995.

Pennsylvania Independent College and University Research Center. *Patterns of Success After College: Labor Market Conditions and Outcomes for Recent Baccalaureate Recipients from Independent Colleges and Universities in Pennsylvania.* Harrisburg: Pennsylvania Independent College and University Research Center, 1997.

MICHAEL D. MCGUIRE is director of the Office of Planning and Institutional Research at Georgetown University.

JASON P. CASEY is director of research for the Association of Independent Colleges and Universities of Pennsylvania.

Define what you want to know that can make a difference; look for assistance; design research projects; understand results; take action; test for improvements; and stay in touch with the field of alumni research. The lessons contained in this volume point the way to alumni research that can lead to action and improvements; this chapter shows how one conference participant implemented an action agenda.

Now What Should You Do?

Joseph Pettit

After reading the earlier chapters, you may ask yourself what you should do now. We thought the best advice we could give would be to tell you how we have *begun* to use what we learned from the various chapters, the other papers presented at the conference, and conference discussions, and how we have applied at least some of this new knowledge.

One of the lessons we learned is that potential users of alumni research and the researchers themselves need to talk to one another more often. More than once during the conference, we heard how organizational structures limit conversations between potential users of alumni research and researchers in other parts of the college or university. At Georgetown, it had been several years since staff from the institutional research office and the university's alumni association had collaborated on a research project. As a result of the conference and subsequent conversations with members of the university's alumni and fundraising staff, two projects evolved. The first attempted to answer a question the parents of our undergraduate students identified in an earlier survey as very important to them: What do graduates do after college? The second involved studying our alumni records to see the extent to which we could replicate the analysis of alumni giving patterns described in the chapter by Joseph S. Collins, William J. Hecht, and Diana Tilley Strange of MIT.

Three opportunities exist for learning what Georgetown's graduates do after college. Shortly before they graduate, seniors complete a survey that asks them, among other things, what they plan to do in the fall after graduation. Then each fall, our career center sends these same graduates a survey that asks them to let us know what they are actually doing. Finally, our alumni association regularly contacts alumni in order to stay current with their home and business addresses and their occupations.

A recent survey of our parents showed they are very interested in what our graduates do both immediately after graduation and in the longer term. Because individual parents are really interested in knowing the careers their own children are likely to enter, it is important to look at careers by the undergraduate majors of the alumni. Finally, we wanted to see whether we could compare the careers of our graduates with those of all college graduates in the country.

From our 1998 senior survey, we learned that the anticipated postgraduation activities varied by academic majors as shown in Table 6.1.

From the career center survey, we found that most graduates followed through with the plans they had during the spring. An analysis of our undergraduate alumni records found that over 50 percent of our alumni give us a business address, but we have occupational codes for only 15 percent. Nevertheless, this meant that we knew the occupations of over seven thousand of our undergraduate alumni. This preliminary analysis, however, suggested our first set of follow-up actions—to examine our procedures for gathering and updating occupational data and to find ways to let alumni know why their occupational data are important to the university. See Table 6.2.

Table 6.1 reveals very different activities for new graduates, depending on their majors, and Table 6.2 shows a similar pattern. Table 6.2 also shows a preponderance of lawyers (except for science majors). Perhaps there is something in the Washington, D.C., air or water! A more likely explanation for the large share of lawyers is the fact that Georgetown University has a large nationally ranked law school. Although fewer than 10 percent of our law school's graduates are also graduates of one of the university's undergraduate schools, one in six of our undergraduate alumni who become lawyers graduate from our law center. Finally, Table 6.2 reveals an absence of Georgetown alumni in service and craft occupations, shown in the bottom portion of the table. Though—given the university's selective admissions—one would expect the representation of our alumni in these occupational fields to be low, we may also be seeing the results of respondent bias; that is, our alumni in these occupations are less likely to supply this information.

Now that we have these profiles, and similar ones for individual majors, what will we do with them? Because the impetus for the research came from

Table 6.1. Plans for Fall

	Humanities (%)	Social Sciences (%)	Natural Sciences/Math (%)	Business (%)
Employment	70	72	40	88
Graduate or professional school	19	21	43	6
Completely undecided	6	3	9	3
Other activity	6	3	9	4

Note: Percentages do not add up to 100 due to rounding.

Table 6.2. Occupational Profile of College Graduates in the United States Compared with Georgetown University Undergraduate Alumni

Occupational Fields	All U.S. College Grads. (%)	All GU Undergraduate Alumni (%)[a]	GU Undergraduate Alumni by Major			
			Humanities (%)	Social Sciences (%)	Natural Sciences/Math (%)	Business (%)
Executive, administrative, and managerial occupations	26	26	20	26	7	51
Administrators and officials, public administrators	1	6	6	9	3	2
Accountants and auditors	3	3	1	1	1	14
Other financial officers	1	10	7	12	1	25
Other executive, administrative, and managerial	20	6	5	4	2	9
Professional specialty occupations	43	68	74	69	91	41
Engineers	4	1	0	0	2	1
Computer analysts, scientists	3	2	2	2	1	2
Natural scientists	2	0	0	1	1	0
Physicians	2	10	5	3	70	1
Teachers: higher education	4	2	4	2	3	0
Teachers: K–12	10	5	12	5	2	1
Lawyers	3	29	25	40	4	21
Other professional specialists	15	20	25	16	7	15
Technicians, including programmers	3	0	0	1	1	0
Sales occupations	11	5	6	4	1	8
Administrative support	8	0	0	0	0	0
Service workers	3	0	0	0	0	0
Farming	1	0	0	0	0	0
Precision production, craft, and repair	3	0	0	0	0	0
Operators and laborers	3	0	0	0	0	0
Total	100	100	100	100	100	100

Note: GU = Georgetown University

[a]The national study and the Georgetown University analysis exclude military occupations. Also, percentages for majors do not add up to all-GU percentages in all cases because of rounding.

Sources: Report on the American Workforce, U.S. Department of Labor, 1997, Tables 1–6, pp. 38–40; personal communication from Dan Hecker, Bureau of Labor Statistics, June 3, 1998; Georgetown University data from a May 1998 extract of all alumni records

responses to a parents' survey, we included information from Tables 6.1 and 6.2 in an article on the services of our university in the fall 1998 *Parents' Newsletter.* We also reported the results to the chairs of academic departments and directors of programs, so they could share the information with their faculty and students. Finally, as noted earlier, we realized that we will have to give continued attention to improving the quality of information on occupational data in our alumni records.

The second research project to emerge from the conference was an examination of our alumni giving patterns, using the MIT methodology. What percentage of our alumni, by undergraduate and graduate programs, make a financial gift to the university in a given year? What percentage of the donors in a given year contributed in the previous year? In their chapter, Collins, Hecht, and Strange report that MIT's Alumni Fund participation rates during the 1970s varied between 40 and 50 percent for alumni whose first MIT degree was a bachelor's, compared with 28 to 32 percent for those whose first degree was a graduate degree. It was during this period that MIT began to supplement an analysis of participation rates with data on patterns of giving. Specifically, they were interested in two questions: How likely is an alumnus who donates in one year to contribute in the following year? Of nonrepeat donors, how likely are they to become donors in years beyond the next one? The MIT research indicated that about 80 percent of the donors in one year become donors in the subsequent year, and that this "conversion" rate declines in each subsequent year that donors fail to contribute again. Of course, this makes intuitive sense, but the key is whether, and how, you modify your fundraising practices to capitalize on the insight.

At Georgetown University, we have only recently begun to conduct regular and systematic analyses of alumni giving patterns. In the past, our focus had been on total dollars received, both overall and from alumni. In fiscal year 1984, our alumni contributed just under $7 million dollars, whereas in fiscal year 1997, the alumni contributed almost $29 million. Although the MIT methodology of examining giving patterns was known to our fundraising staff, our past efforts had been focused on building the administrative and information systems and on the demands of a capital campaign. These efforts preempted research on giving patterns and discussions of how such research might cause us to change our fundraising practices. With new systems and personnel in place and the capital campaign successfully launched, the alumni research conference was an opportunity for collaboration between staff in the alumni association and in the planning and institutional research office.

The 1997 report of the Council for Aid to Education reveals that the *solicitation effectiveness rate* (donors as a percentage of alumni asked to give for any purpose) at MIT was 38 percent compared with 24 percent for all private research-doctoral universities; Georgetown's rate was 20 percent. As at MIT, alumni whose first degree from Georgetown was a bachelor's were more likely to contribute than those whose first Georgetown degree was a graduate degree. Similarly, repeat donors showed the same patterns as those at MIT, although at lower rates, reflecting the lower participation—or solicitation effectiveness—rates.

More important than the data will be the conversations about the implications of these differences in participation rates and giving patterns for our fundraising practices. How can solicitations tied to class reunions be conducted so as to maximize the likelihood of a repeat contribution the following year? What additional research could help fundraisers and volunteer leaders understand which changes would be most worthwhile? Should annual goals for groups of alumni (undergraduate, graduate, law and medicine) include dollars, and participation rates, both overall and by repeat givers? Conversations that address these questions will undoubtedly lead to more action-oriented research. Plans are already being formulated to follow Jerold Pearson's lead at Stanford in probing involvement with and feelings toward one's alma mater. Future planning will also focus on developing a multipurpose alumni survey tied to reunion cycles.

The present state of research on college and university alumni was best captured by one of the conference's discussants, David Davis-Van Atta, director of institutional research at Carleton College:

> Within the next few years, I believe we will begin to develop a body of research-based knowledge about a variety of important issues related to alumni and development. From these findings, we will develop better understandings of the commonalities across various types of institutions, and patterns in the differences among them. However, at present, we do not have this body of knowledge nor depth and detail of understanding in the alumni-development area. As a result, for now, and for some time to come, it will be best to do one's own research. . . . At this time I see institutional research, with respect to work in the area of alumni and development, at essentially the same point IR was with respect to admissions-related market research somewhere around the early 1980s.

Knowledge of what other researchers of alumni have learned is crucial to maximizing the effectiveness of alumni research. Besides this volume, the Council for the Advancement and Support of Education (CASE) has published a summary of all the papers and discussions at the 1998 Alumni Research Conference. (*Research in Alumni Relations: Report on the 1998 AIR-CASE Alumni Research Conference* can be ordered by calling (800) 554–8536 and requesting item 28124.) Additional AIR-CASE alumni research conferences are being planned. Watch for announcements in the *Electronic AIR* and *CASE Currents*. An alumni research special-interest group will meet annually at the AIR forum, and the CASE annual meeting will include presentations from the AIR-CASE conferences. The research and discussions these conferences promote should bring a new era to alumni research.

JOSEPH PETTIT is vice president for planning and institutional research and the class of '64 communications chair at Georgetown University.

INDEX

Back Issue/Subscription Order Form

Copy or detach and send to:
Jossey-Bass Inc., Publishers, 350 Sansome Street, San Francisco CA 94104-1342

Call or fax toll free!
Phone 888-378-2537 6AM-5PM PST; Fax 800-605-2665

Back issues   Please send me the following issues at $23 each:
(Important: please include series initials and issue number, such as IR90)

1. IR _____

_____

_____

$ _____ Total for single issues

$ _____ Shipping charges (for single issues *only;* subscriptions are exempt from shipping charges): Up to $30, add $5^{50} • $30^{01}–$50, add $6^{50} $50^{01}–$75, add $7^{50} • $75^{01}–$100, add $9 • $100^{01}–$150, add $10 Over $150, call for shipping charge

Subscriptions   Please ❑ start   ❑ renew my subscription to *New Directions for Institutional Research* for the year 1999 at the following rate:

❑ Individual $56   ❑ Institutional $95
NOTE: Subscriptions are quarterly, and are for the calendar year only. Subscriptions begin with the spring issue of the year indicated above. For shipping outside the U.S., please add $25.

$ _____ Total single issues and subscriptions (CA, IN, NJ, NY and DC residents, add sales tax for single issues. NY and DC residents must include shipping charges when calculating sales tax. NY and Canadian residents only, add sales tax for subscriptions.)

❑ Payment enclosed (U.S. check or money order only)

❑ VISA, MC, AmEx, Discover Card #_____ Exp. date_____

Signature _____ Day phone _____

❑ Bill me (U.S. institutional orders only. Purchase order required.)

Purchase order #_____

Name _____

Address _____

_____

_____

Phone_____ E-mail _____

For more information about Jossey-Bass Publishers, visit our Web site at:
www.josseybass.com   **PRIORITY CODE = ND1**

OTHER TITLES AVAILABLE IN THE
NEW DIRECTIONS FOR INSTITUTIONAL RESEARCH SERIES
J. Fredericks Volkwein, Editor-in-Chief